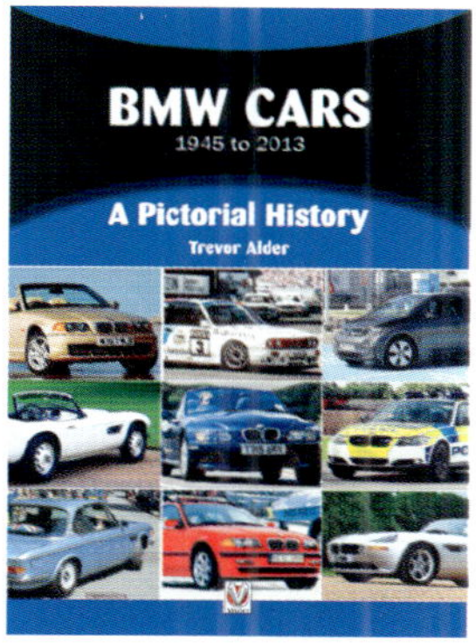
BMW CARS
1945 to 2013
A Pictorial History
Trevor Alder

A Pictorial History – more titles in this series

Austin Cars 1948 to 1990 (Rowe)
Bentley Cars (Taylor)
Citroën Cars 1934 to 1986 (Parish)
Ford Cars – Ford UK cars 1945-1995 (Rowe)
Lotus Cars 1952 to 2024 (Vale)
Jaguar Cars 1946 to 2008 (Thorley)
Mercedes Benz Cars 1947 to 2000 (Taylor)
MG Cars 1930 to 2006 (Alder)
Morris Cars 1948 to 1984 (Newell)
Riley & Wolseley Cars 1948 to 1975 (Rowe)
Rootes Cars of the 50s, 60s & 70s (Hillman, Humber, Singer, Sunbeam & Talbot) (Rowe)
Rover Cars 1945 to 2005 (Taylor)
Saab Cars 1949 to 2011 (Parish)
Triumph & Standard Cars 1945 to 1984 (Warrington)
Vauxhall Cars 1945 to 1995 (Alder)
Volvo Cars 1945 to 1995 (Alder)

More BMW titles

BMW Classic 5 Series (Cranswick)
BMW M3 & M4 (Robson)
BMW E30 3 Series: How to modify for High-Performance and Competition (Hosier)

Essential Buyer's Guides

BMW X5 (Saunders)
BMW Z3 Roadster 1995 to 2002 (Fishwick)

www.veloce.co.uk

First published in 2025 by Veloce, an imprint of David and Charles Limited. Tel +44 (0)1305 260068 / e-mail info@veloce.co.uk / web www.veloce.co.uk.
ISBN: 9781836440031 Readers with ideas for automotive books, or books on other transport or related hobby subjects, are invited to write to the editorial director of Veloce at the above address. British Library Cataloguing in Publication Data – A catalogue record for this book is available from the British Library. Design and production by Veloce. Printed and bound in the UK by Short Run Press Ltd.

BMW CARS

1945 to 2013

A Pictorial History

Trevor Alder

VELOCE

CONTENTS

INTRODUCTION

BMW has been manufacturing vehicles for over 100 years. Its first motorcycle, the R32, was produced from 1923. Gradually the company grew from strength to strength, and produced industrial aircraft and marine engines in its early days. After obtaining a licence to build a series of cars based on the Austin Seven design in the late 1920s, the company moved ahead into the sports car market. After turning to help in the war effort, it bravely took on high-specification luxury car building in the early 1950s.

By the mid-1950s, something new and radical was needed, and despite continuing cash flow problems, BMW gained permission to build a microcar under licence from Iso in Italy. This lower end of the market diminished after a while, as did the sales of motorcycles, so financial investment was sought and this secured the way forward for initially the 700 and then the New Class range of cars, eventually leading to the present-day worldwide operation.

This book chronicles the BMW car scene pre-war up to around 2013, and includes references to those models that also became available just for overseas markets. Throughout the main chapters, in blue tinted boxes, there are some of the headlines used in contemporary advertising from various sources, including some from overseas. These are certainly not exhaustive (there truly are hundreds for certain models), but I have tried to include every model manufactured where possible, however some, such as the quirky little Z1, had no press adverts at all. What became clear during the compilation of this book was that virtually every model has some sort of sporting version, of which each has its unique following.

BMW is an abbreviation for Bayerische Motoren Werke (Bavarian Motor Works in English).

The book is divided into logical chapters, and within these are specific model histories, key production changes, a brief overview of specifications, performance, and a variety of photographs, many of them period, that hopefully serve as a useful guide to the post-war history of BMW cars.

The book does not include motorcycles other than those mentioned that were used in the development of certain cars.

Thanks to BMW for the use of some of the photos, and the many owners and enthusiasts I have spoken to. The BMW museum in Munich is worth a visit, too, with a number of very interesting exhibits of cars, motorcycles and microcars.

Trevor Alder

Line drawings © Trevor Alder, 2025

"It takes one to catch one." (1974 UK advertisement)

PRE-WAR TO 1941 – BMW'S EARLY DAYS

Bayerische Motoren Werke was busy in large marine and aircraft engine production throughout the 1920s, but soon branched into much smaller internal combustion engines for industrial use. The natural progression was to move to motorcycle engines and then to complete bikes, including the inaugural R32, which made its debut at the Paris Show in 1923. This was followed by ever expanding motorcycle production, and it was not until the early 1930s that a BMW badge was seen on a motor car.

Several bikes were designed and built, including the R37 and R63, which went on to win the Grand Prix of Luxembourg and a gold medal in the International Six Days Trial in the UK. More were entered and this strategy did a sterling job in securing much needed sales; there were 573 victories in the 1923-1928 period. Sales were at a record level by the end of 1927, with 27,875 motorcycles sold, ensuring the company was in a strong place financially. Aircraft engine production continued and, by 1930, 1000 Type VI engines had been produced. Management had been keen to expand again and looked at the automobile industry.

When the company acquired the new Dixi works at Eisenach, it embarked on the production of a version of the Austin Seven under licence from the UK. In March 1929 the DA-2 became the first car to wear the BMW roundel. Following this, BMW offered a range of newly designed, high quality, yet smaller sports and touring cars at the lower end of the market, so as not to upset Daimler-Benz, which was a major BMW stockholder. A BMW Dixi DA-3 Wartburg Sport was produced between 1930 and 1931 with the traditional 748cc capacity and could reach 59mph.

In 1932 the DA-4 was the last BMW to be based on the Austin Seven, but incorporated swing axle front independent suspension. Overall, 18,976 automobiles were sold from 1929 through to the end of the 3/15 Series. Unlike their predecessors, the new 300 series models that followed were entirely engineered in Munich, with no association with Austin at all. The sections that follow cover the rather confusing number system adopted by BMW in the 1930s.

BMW 315 on the Rallye Balkanique.

315, 319, 320, 321 & 329

The first of the 300 series was the 315, of which 9765 were produced between 1934 and 1937. It was available as a tourer, sports tourer, saloon, sports saloon, cabriolet, cabriolet limousine and a drophead coupé. Power was from a six-cylinder OHV 1490cc engine with four-speed synchromesh manual gearbox. It was also marketed in the UK as a Frazer Nash BMW Type 34, and could also be ordered with a triple-carburettor arrangement. The 80mph 315/1 derivative was an attractive two-seat sports car version with a choice of a larger engine (a 1911cc six-cylinder unit), and 242 were produced, all with drum brakes. Frazer Nash of Isleworth, London, also converted some of these into right-hand drive for the UK market between 1937 and 1939, and branded them Frazer Nash BMW. AFN Ltd was the official importer to the UK.

Between 1935 and 1937, 6646 type 319 cars were manufactured. Almost identical in appearance to the 315, the 319 boasted the larger engine of the 315/1 (1911cc 45bhp six-cylinder), and, once again, triple carburettors could be ordered. 100 examples were made, and UK magazine *The Light Car* called it "a wolf in sheep's clothing."

In 1937, the 315 and 319 were replaced by the shorter-chassis 320, built with a

Le Mans, 1939, and the 328 Touring coupé.

box-section frame and hydraulic brakes. This lasted until 1939, when replaced by the 321, which had wider section tyres but appeared identical externally. This model continued to be produced post-war and was known as the Awtowelo.

The 329 was a short production run (1936-1937) cabriolet and sports cabriolet based on the 319 mechanicals, but achieved 1170 in sales numbers. Overall, its appearance looked like the 320 and it had cable-operated brakes.

326 & 327

The 326 was a large 113in wheelbase four-door design in either saloon or cabriolet form, with a two-door cabriolet also available. This was the first vehicle in the 300 family to feature a live rear axle and torsion bars, and made its debut at the 1936 Berlin Motor Show. Power came from a six-cylinder, 1971cc unit, and 15,949 cars were produced.

The lower and more streamlined 327/80 and 327/55 were based on the 326 frame (shortened), engine, suspension and brakes. In total, 1396 and 569 were produced respectively, all two-seaters as either a fixed-head coupé or cabriolet. Post-war, it continued from East Germany as the EMW.

328

Around 450 328 two-seat models were produced between 1936 and 1939, again with the six-cylinder 1971cc engine. These are highly sought after today and capable of up to 100mph on the autobahn. The model had a twin-tubed frame and semi-elliptic suspension at the rear. A special Beutler-bodied 328 certainly looked ahead of its years when built in 1937. Bespoke streamlined versions of the 328 were entered into the 1938 Mille Miglia event in Italy and a whole fleet entered the 1938 German Grand Prix. The Le Mans event

BMW 327 coupé (1937-1941).

BMW 328 at the Silvretta Classic Rally in 2014.

also featured the BMW 328, both standard and streamlined, and the latter would record faster speeds than its sister cars down the Mulsanne Straight.

As with the 315, Frazer Nash of Isleworth, London also converted the 328 into right-hand drive, and it sold well in the UK. After the war, the 328 continued, not in manufacture, but collecting trophies for its continued racing success. Frazer Nash continued with a very streamlined 328 that set the tone for other streamlined racers such as the Jaguar XK.

In 1947, another UK firm, the Bristol Aeroplane company, used various pre-war BMW designs and parts to produce an impressive cousin car: the Bristol 400 – a luxurious combination of 327 two-door bodywork, 328 pushrod engine and 326 chassis. Bristol followed this with its revised models and body types through the 1950s, culminating in the 407, which had an American engine.

335

Produced at the outbreak of the Second World War, the big 90hp 335 was a large luxury saloon or cabriolet on two- and four-door platforms on a 117in wheelbase. It featured a 3.5-litre in-line six-cylinder engine coupled to a ZF all-synchromesh gearbox and was good for 90mph. After the outbreak of war in September 1939, the factory's priority changed, and just 410 were manufactured, with production never resuming. Some examples made their way to the UK by personal importation after the war, mainly by ex-forces personnel.

After the war broke out, production switched to military motorcycle manufacture, and around 16,000 R75 bikes were produced, along with the BMW 325 4x4 military truck. Aircraft engines were also seen again, with V12s being supplied for the Messerschmitt Bf 109 fighter aircraft. BMW also took over Bramo in Brandenburg for the manufacture of rocket engines for missiles.

BMW 335 four-door cabriolet.

1952-1959 – 501, 502, 503 & 507

501 & 502: The Baroque Angel

The 501 photographed when new.

The BMW 501 was the first new BMW to be produced after the war, and it debuted at the Frankfurt Motor Show in April 1951, when a pre-production prototype was displayed. Production would not get under way until October 1952 due to delays in body production. The first 2045 cars were manufactured by Karosserie Baur to enable production to start while BMW was tooling up elsewhere for higher production numbers. The two-litre pushrod engine was virtually the same as the pre-war 326's unit, but now with a Solex carburettor with two-position starting device. Now that front leaf springs were no longer used, the engine was moved further forward compared with pre-war cars, improving cabin space. A four-speed ZF all-synchromesh gearbox, mounted under the rear seats, also improved interior room as there was no transmission tunnel, but was ingeniously linked under the floor to an American-style column gearchange. Everything else was new, including a hefty welded frame of brand-new design, with a front section that supported the engine and suspension, and separate rear outer section that included the body mounts and rear suspension which comprised very long longitudinal torsion bars.

The four-door saloon body styling was certainly groundbreaking, and a little controversial. The front end resembled the pre-war 327 with a tall upright twin grille. However, the rest of the styling was groundbreaking, using curved-glass technology. The windscreen used a distinct and attractive wraparound curve, the screen was now fixed in position and no longer openable. Running boards, still seen on post-war cars, were no longer used, and all panels took on a swooping, curved line, including the roofline that descended towards the rear of the car. All panels at the rear were also curved, as was the rear bumper, like the front, and the rear screen too, although the earliest 501s had a smaller rear screen that was non wraparound. The rear passenger doors were hinged at the rear, and body colours were somewhat limited, as with Henry Ford's quote, "You can have any colour you like, as long as it's black." Strong new post-war competition

The 501 sedan (left), and the 501 in two-door cabriolet form (right).

The front running gear of the 501 as displayed at Motor Shows.

came from Ford, Opel, Borgward, DKW and Daimler-Benz; the 501 was going to have to be a strong contender to be successful. The car was nicknamed the Baroque Angel due to its distinctive, flowing contours.

Internal appointments were good, although the switchgear and knobs were spread around the cabin, making them not particularly easy to identify and use. It was entirely possible to seat six occupants inside the wider body, albeit with no elbow room. There were two separate front seats (and each one reclined separately) but with virtually no room between them, hence three up front and three behind.

The performance of the six-cylinder cars was hardly scorching, but Ernst Loof won the 2-litre class outright in a 1953 Nürburgring race event on home soil followed that same year by another outright class win in the *Tour de Belgique* against 161 competitors. However, the expensive 501's sales were not as high as expected, with the public still largely travelling by two wheels, not four, and average annual earnings only one quarter of what this model cost. The Mercedes-Benz 220 was only two thirds of its price, slightly quicker, but there were waiting lists, whereas the BMW was ex-stock.

The more powerful V8 502 models were available from the 1955 model year, and continued in production until 1963, with some models being right-hand drive and fitted with wood veneer and leather trim and a floor gear lever. Servo-assisted brakes were offered on deluxe models, with very late cars gaining front disc brakes, too.

The V8 was largely thanks to the return to BMW of Fritz Fiedler, who had done a stint at Bristol and Frazer Nash in the UK, returning for a brief spell at Opel before settling back at BMW. The 2580cc engine used a light-alloy block and heads with a two-barrel downdraught Solex carburettor. The 502 made its debut at the Geneva Salon in March 1954.

Two variations of the 501 were also offered at this time, the 501A and 501B, both now equipped with an improved-performance version of the 1971cc engine, with the B version available in lesser trim form with a hefty price reduction of 1500 DM, which improved sales substantially. In the spring of 1955, the original six-cylinder engine was enlarged to 2077cc via a 2mm bore increase to 68mm. There was also a cheaper, detuned version of the 2.6-litre 502 known as the 501 V8. Extra brightwork was fitted to the 502 from 1955.

Production of the six-cylinder model lasted until 1958 as the 501/3, while the V8 cars continued until the end of production in 1963, and some had a more powerful 3168cc V8

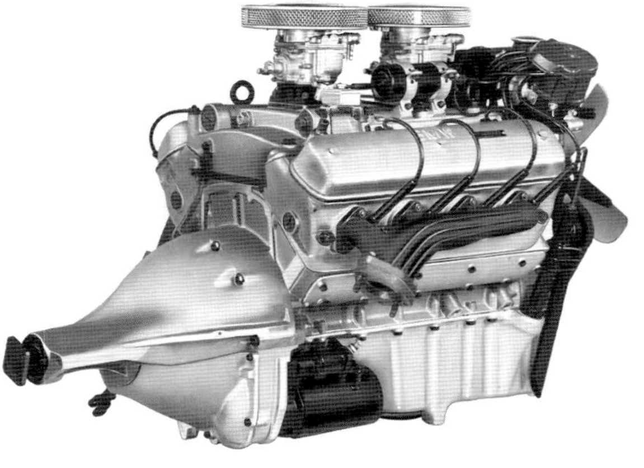

The 502/503 V8 3168cc engine.

The 502 saloon.

engine first seen at the Frankfurt Motor Show in 1955. This model was simply known as the BMW 3.2, while the smaller-engine car was known as the 2.6. The larger V8 did have better performance; 0-60mph was now around 15 seconds. An even faster 502 was the 3.2 Super (140bhp) from 1957 and, towards the end of production, improvements included the option of power steering and front disc brakes with vacuum-boost assistance. Final run-out models were known as the 2600 and 3200, each offered with two trim versions: the L (Luxus) and the S (Super). The 160bhp 3200S uniquely used twin Zenith carburettors and was reported as being the fastest production saloon built in Germany at the time, achieving a top speed approaching 120mph. Just 1328 of these were manufactured.

Two-door coupé and convertible variants of the 501 and 502 series were available but not through the factory. Coachbuilders Autenrieth of Darmstadt and Baur of Stuttgart produced factory-approved conversions, with Autenrieth introducing styling changes such as a lowered bonnet, more raked front grille and squared wheelarches. As for long-wheelbase conversions, a high-roofed ambulance version of the 502 was built by Heidemann and just two examples of a 505 model in limousine form were manufactured in 1955, with a staggering UK price approaching nearly £2700.

The facia of the 502 coupé.

Styled by Michelotti, it used the 120hp 3.2-litre V8, and the 1955 Frankfurt show car is now in the BMW museum. Frazer Nash also fitted the V8 engines into some competition cars, with production halting in 1957.

501 AND 502 BODY TYPES: Four-door saloon plus some specialist conversions and a coupé. **Manufactured at:** Munich. **Number produced:** 8951 501s and 13,500 V8 cars. **Production span:** 1952-1963.
TOP SPEED: 84mph/135km/h (2-litre) and 120mph/185km/h (3.2 V8); **0-60mph/100km/h:** 27 seconds (two-litre) 15 seconds (3.2 V8); **average economy:** 23-28mpg (six-cylinder cars); 15-20mpg (V8).
PRICE AT LAUNCH: 15;000 new DM
MEASUREMENTS: Length: 15ft 6¼in (4.73m); **height:** 5ft ½in (1.53m); **wheelbase:** 9ft 3½in (2.83m); **width:** 5ft 10in (1.78m); **kerb weight:** 3153lb (1430kg); **wheels:** 16in; **turning circle:** 36ft 3in (11.0m); **fuel capacity:** 12.75 gallons/58 litres; **boot capacity:** "Five suitcases."
TECHNICAL: Engine types: 1971 and 2077cc six-cylinder and 2580 and 3168cc V8 petrol; **gearbox:** four-speed manual; **suspension:** upper and lower A-arms with longitudinal torsion bar each side (front); two longitudinal torsion bars (rear); **brakes:** drum front (front disc optional on late V8 cars) and drum rear.
TRIM: Cloth/leather.
KEY OPTIONAL EXTRAS: Power steering (late V8 cars only).

501 and 502 advertising slogans
For the discerning motorist (501, 1957)
Fur hohere Anspruche (501, 1956 German)
Der personliche stil … (501, 502 German)

503

In the late 1950s, BMW's sales strategy was to produce two ranges of cars at each end of the price spectrum. The microcars took on the entry-level position, while the expensive 501/502 was complemented by two exotic V8 sports cars the company had high hopes for in the American market. In 1954, dealers over the water suggested they could sell as many V8 sports cars as BMW could make, but in the event, production of the 503 was delayed from the outset, which disheartened American buyers and the car never enjoyed the sales success hoped for. On the plus side, here was a stunning two-door sports model styled by Albrecht Goertz (he had previously worked on the styling of the Studebakers) with all-alloy bodywork and, for cost savings, the running gear came from the existing large saloons. A prototype was shown to the public at the 1955 Frankfurt Motor Show, and production followed in May 1956. The four-seat 503 was available as a cabriolet and hardtop coupé.

In late 1956, the huge £4463 retail price of the new 503 was very similar to the 300 SL Mercedes-Benz (£4651), and this price towered above Coventry's Jaguar XK140 (£1741), and even surpassed the Jaguar D-Type (£3878). In fact the 503 was so exclusive, only the Rolls-Royce range of cars in the UK remained more expensive.

Its styling, with a traditional vertical grille ahead of a long bonnet, was not to everyone's taste. Although looking very Italian from the front, overall the bodywork lacked zest, with slab sides and no flair. Its two-seat stablemate 507 certainly had the styling advantage. A power-operated fabric hood was welcomed, as were the electric windows, but a poor column change on this model proved unpopular, being replaced by a standard floor lever from 1957. Today, however, the 503 is highly collectable.

503 BODY TYPES: Coupé and cabriolet. **Manufactured at:** Munich. **Number produced:** 412. **Production span:** 1956-1959.
PERFORMANCE: Top speed: 118mph/190km/h; **0-60mph/100km/h:** 12 seconds; **average economy:** 15-20mpg.
PRICE AT LAUNCH: £4463 17s.
MEASUREMENTS: Length: 15ft 6¼in (4.73m); **height:** 5ft ½in (1.53m); **width:** 5ft 7in (1.7m); **wheelbase:** 9ft 3½in (2.83m); **kerb weight:** 3220lb (1460kg); **wheels:** 16in; **turning circle:** 36ft 5in (11.1m); **fuel capacity:** 16½ gallons/75 litres; **boot capacity:** very small.
TECHNICAL: Engine types: 3168cc V8 petrol; **gearbox:** four-speed manual; **suspension:** double wishbones and torsion bars (front); live axle and torsion bars (rear); **brakes:** hydraulically assisted drum front and rear.
TRIM: Leather.

The 503 coupe photographed in 2005.

The 503 interior, this one has been fully restored.

507

A very interesting quote from US *Car and Driver* magazine in a 1959 test stated, "The 507's strongest appeal is its beauty. No other car has such animal grace or more justifies the old expression "it looks like it's going a hundred when it's standing still." The front-end styling was completely different to the 503, with a flattened twin-kidney grille, which gave it an aggressive stance and lower bonnet line. This model, hand-built on a shortened 501/502 chassis, had been designed alongside the larger 503 as a two-seat sports model of high pedigree and was launched at the same time. Production was, however, some six months behind the 503, starting in November 1956.

Its body panels were individually beaten from aluminium sheet by the Bavarian craftsmen, and it surely must pass as one of the most beautiful two-seat sports cars of the 1950s. With its 150hp 3.2-litre V8, the model could whisk to 60mph in just around ten seconds through its twin-carburettor setup. Americans were expecting to see it at around $5000, but when it arrived, after slow production, it cost $9000 and sales were slower than expected. Hoffman, the American dealer which had encouraged the whole project, was quick to offer 12,000 DM for 2000 units delivered, but this had failed to materialise given its final price. Just 250 were produced, all in left-hand drive form.

A 507 is displayed when brand new.

A pristine 507 photographed in modern days – note the BMW bike at the back!

Just the thing to get you fast to the airport – another 507.

It quickly became apparent the luggage compartment was too small, especially when the spare wheel was carried, so a smaller fuel tank could be ordered to allow for better boot capacity. However, along with the 503, production was halted in March of 1959 despite some very favourable American road test reports being published, and the entire programme had not been cost-effective at all. In October 1959 the Munich press department loaned a spare 507 to UK's *Autocar* magazine, which had been keen to get one for testing, but to no avail. The test went from Munich on an Alpine route of several hundred miles south through Austria, Switzerland and Italy, covering many of the famous passes before they closed for the winter, then back north to Munich. Sadly, this single three-page account appears to be the only contemporary driving report ever published in a UK magazine and concentrated more on the spectacular route than on the performance or problems encountered with the vehicle.

507 BODY TYPES: Roadster hardtop coupé. **Manufactured at:** Munich. **Number produced:** 250. **Production span:** 1956-1959. **PERFORMANCE: Top speed:** 129mph/207 km/h; **0-60mph/100km/h:** 9 seconds; **average economy:** 14-18mpg. **PRICE AT LAUNCH:** £4201 11s. **MEASUREMENTS: Length:** 14ft 6¼in (4.42m); **height:** 4ft 4½in (1.33m); **width:** 5ft 5in (1.65m); **wheelbase:** 8ft 1½in (2.48m);

A pristine 507 photographed in 2003. All 507s were left-hand drive.

kerb weight: 3220lb (1460kg); **wheels:** 16in; **turning circle:** 36ft 5in (11.1m); **fuel capacity:** 18.5 US gallons; **boot capacity:** very minimal.

TECHNICAL: Engine types: 3168cc V8-cylinder petrol; **gearbox:** four-speed manual; **suspension:** double wishbones and torsion bars (front), live axle and torsion bars (rear); **brakes:** hydraulically assisted drums front and rear, except last few models with front disc.

TRIM: Leather.

OPTIONAL EXTRAS: Smaller fuel tank to allow greater fuel capacity, removable hardtop roof, Rudge Whitworth knock-off wheels.

507 advertising slogans

You'd be surprised what a BMW convertible is going for these days (507, 1995)
Europe's leading V8 (507, 1956)
Kultur auf Redern (1916-1958) German, 501-7

ISETTA, 600 & 700

Isetta – the rolling egg

After the Second World War, money was scarce everywhere, and having any motor vehicle was deemed a luxury. As the years continued, and with the extensive rail network going through so many cuts, many families progressed into a motorcycle and sidecar combination that bridged a gap between two-wheel transport and running a car. It was quite common to see a family of four – adults on the bike, and the children in the sidecar with all their holiday luggage crammed in alongside – making their way to the coast in the summer.

The microcar evolved and tapped a definite gap in the market with a much needed drier method of transport. Many European firms offered some delightful contraptions during the 1950s in three- and four-wheel forms. With the impossibly narrow city streets seen in Italian cities, Iso developed its little Isetta by 1953 and it was produced in a variety of interesting guises for passenger and goods transportation. With the new Fiat 500 looming, the Isetta took a sales dive in its Italian home market, resulting in it being offered out by Iso to be built under licence in various European countries including France, Belgium, Spain and, of course, Germany.

A licence was also granted for the Romi-Isetta in Brazil. Iso's main business was building motor scooters and tiny three-wheel utility trucks, the type often seen in markets and outside railway stations, not to mention its refrigerator production. Eventually, using the profits from the microcar licences, Iso built its superb Rivolta IR300 sports car of 1963. Iso was looking for a licence agreement with Germany and a deal was soon struck with BMW. The BMW version of the Isetta was produced from April 1955. However, BMW not only bought the licence to build these cars, but also the factory tooling, which proved favourable, as production could be brought

Enjoying the sunshine with the fabric roof open on an Isetta.

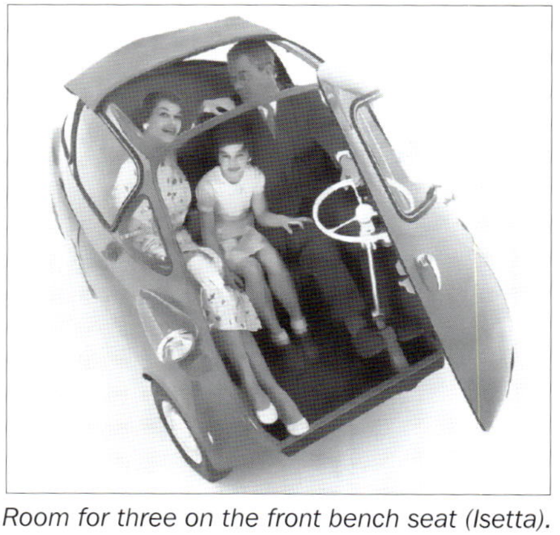

Room for three on the front bench seat (Isetta).

Isetta on the beach. With the roof open, long loads could be carried, perhaps not the boat though …

The front door swings open wide (600). Note the clever design of the steering column.

ahead quite considerably. They were produced quickly and efficiently; over 10,000 were made by the end of that calendar year.

Essentially a four-wheeler with a very narrow 20in rear track with no differential, this bubble-shaped two-plus-one (small child only) single-bench-seat vehicle soon won the hearts of many, characterised by its swing-out front end which, when opened, took the steering wheel and column with it. Some models without any reverse gear facility caused panic if parking next to a brick wall, with exiting only possible via the canvas roof! Power was by way of the tiny home-built 12hp 245cc R45 motorcycle engine (a single-cylinder two-stroke 236cc engine produced by Iso proved too smelly, dirty and less favourable, and only achieved a 45mph top speed), then a 13hp 298cc engine driving the rear. The latter engine was borrowed from the existing BMW R27 motorcycle. Acceleration could only be described as a challenge, with a 0-30mph time of around half a minute. The new model soon became known in Germany as 'das rollende ei' (the rolling egg).

In the UK in 1956, the retail price of the Isetta Motocoupe was £292 plus tax, equating to £439 7 shillings. Other microcars were available for the following retail amounts in late 1956:

Bond two-seater	£278 13s
Bond DeLuxe four-seater	£320 4s
Goggomobil T300	£505 7s
Goggomobil Sliding Head	£515 12s

It takes one to catch one!

With relevant engineering changes, the car was also produced under licence from BMW (not Iso this time) as a three-wheeler, still with 10in wheels, by AFN at the old railway site in Brighton, UK, from 1958, and was known as the Isetta 300. Taxation for new cars and road fund licences on three-wheelers was greatly reduced over conventional cars at the time, and around 1750 UK cars were built.

The list of both three- and four-wheel microcars grew steadily in that decade. A further delve into the archives of three-wheeler prices in a very competitive late 1959 UK line-up reveals:

Berkeley two/three-seater	£399 19s
Bond Minicar Family deluxe	£327
Bond Mk F family saloon	£376 8s
Coronet two-seater	£436 13s
Frisky Family Three	£376 6s
Heinkel Cabin Cruiser	£389 9s
Isetta (Standard)	£328 6s
Isetta Plus saloon	£353 9s
Messerschmitt KR200 de luxe	£332 10s
Messerschmitt KR201 Sports convertible	£332 10s
Nobel 200	£385 2s
Reliant Regal coupé MkIV	£434 13s
Reliant Regal hardtop	£434 13s
Scootacar	£287 10s

Ubiquitous UK press advert for the Isetta. £359!

For clarity, Issigonis' new BMC Mini 850, a revolutionary new baby four-seat with four wheels, launched in August 1959, priced £496 19s.

Isetta production continued, with detail modifications made to the teardrop-shaped headlamp pod assemblies from October 1956; these side-mounted units were shortened. A main difference with the later Isettas was the adoption of completely different sliding side glass, also from October 1956, and the option of the slightly larger, 298cc 13hp engine also from that year. The changed side glass took away some of the charming bubble character of the original design, and subsequently the distinctive triangular side front glass pieces and wraparound rear screen were no more. Overall, the revised Isetta was a couple of inches longer.

ISETTA BODY TYPES: One front door, with fabric roof. **Manufactured at:** Munich and Brighton. **Number produced:** 161,728. **Production span:** 1955-1962. **PERFORMANCE:** **Top speed:** 53mph/90km/h;

BMW certainly brought some bright colours into its 1950s microcar range.

Isetta again – note the exhaust vent at the bottom of the body side.

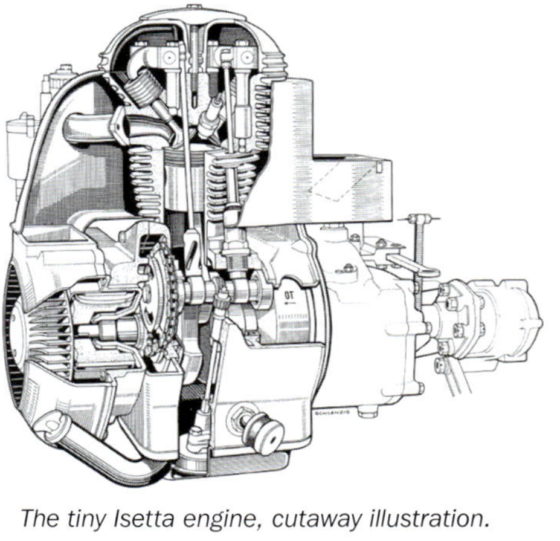

The tiny Isetta engine, cutaway illustration.

Left: Crossing the border at Berlin. Microcars were often used to smuggle people through by cleverly ditching the fuel tank and hiding somebody under a cover. Right, the same Isetta shows the whitewall tyres that were popular at the time.

Left: A UK-manufactured Isetta three-wheeler at the 1960 London Motor Show at Earls Court. Right: Note the longer headlamp covers on this facelift car.

An early press photograph.

0-40mph/65km/h: 40 seconds; **average economy:** 75mpg.
PRICE AT LAUNCH: 2580 DM.
MEASUREMENTS: **Length:** 7ft 6in (2.28m); **height:** 4ft 2½in (1.28m); **width:** 4ft 6in (1.37m); **wheelbase:** 4ft 11½in (1.51m); **kerb weight:** 795lb (361kg); **wheels:** 10in; **turning circle:** 27ft 3in (8.3m); **fuel capacity:** 3½

The Isetta was ideal for any drive-through German market!

Isetta on the production line.

gallons/13 litres; **boot capacity:** 80 litres.
TECHNICAL: Engine types: 247cc and 297cc single-cylinder petrol; **gearbox:** four-speed manual (no automatic ever offered); **suspension:** trailing arms and coil springs (front), leaf-sprung live axle (rear); **brakes:** hydraulically operated drums all round.
TRIM: Vinyl.
KEY OPTIONAL EXTRAS: Chrome luggage rack for the rear, two-tone paint.

Isetta advertising slogans
World's cheapest car to buy and run! (Isetta)
Isetta is in such demand (1957)
8 reasons why the Isetta is in such demand
7½ feet of thrill-packed driving in the sensational Isetta
Great economy car in America (Isetta)
The little miracle with a big heart and a tiny thirst (Isetta)
Knowledgeable people buy Imperial and then they buy it by the case (Isetta)

It takes a keen eye to see this is actually the 600, which had a very similar front end to the Isetta.

An American advert showing the 600's two doors, with one at the side, the other up front.

The 1958 chassis of the 600.

The side without the door on the 600. All production cars were this way.

The 600 four-wheeler

After the introduction of the Isetta, BMW needed a stopgap filler for the void created between its small Isetta and the larger and way more expensive 501 and 502 series. There were no funds available to even consider the design of perhaps a 1.5-litre mid-priced passenger car – that would come in the 1960s. So what appeared was not quite a gap-filler, but more of a larger Isetta. The new 600 four-wheeler had only a slightly narrower rear track but a longer wheelbase, and took up a more efficient rectangle of space than its triangular predecessors. The end result by designer Willy Black was a car 2ft longer than the Isetta – and 2ft shorter than any mainstream new car. To save on design and tooling, many of the components were the same, including use of the chassis, which had simply been extended, and a conventional rear axle allowed for the rear seating.

Launched in December 1957, the new 600 took on the general frontal appearance of the Isetta again with its unique front-opening door and hinged steering column. The door proved a little heavy to open for some folk, with some comments in contemporary road testing stating that the spring counter-balancers were not strong enough for the door to stay physically open, and it was often difficult to alight from the low front seat. As the door now cleverly concealed the spare wheel and tyre, and a more orthodox facia, it was appreciably heavier, which compounded the problem. A larger engine was needed to haul around this four-seat car and, again, BMW took to using one of its motorcycle engines rather than go to a third party or design a new engine. The twin-piston 582cc from the recently discontinued R67 motorcycle was used, giving 19.5hp at 4000rpm, good for around a 60mph top speed. A four-speed

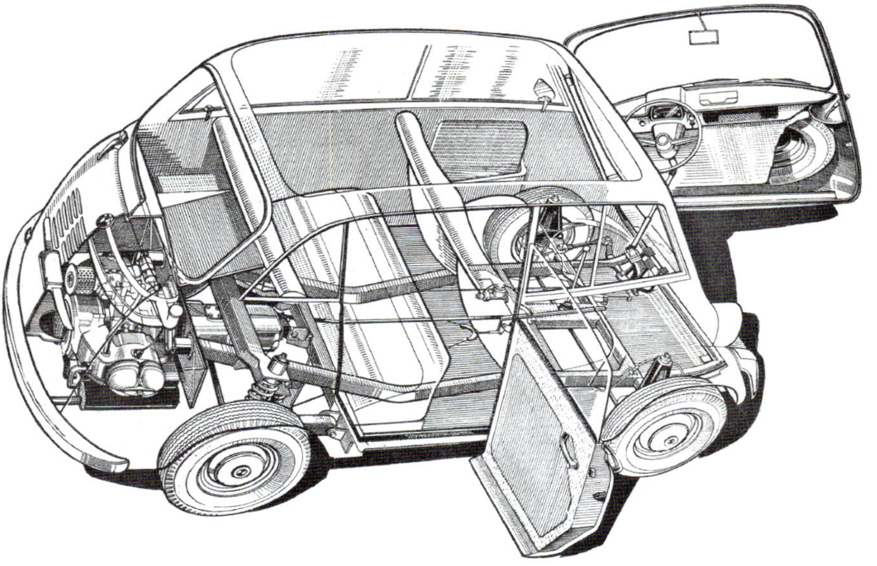

The 600's rear right-hand side aspect in cutaway form.

manual gearbox was mated to this, and stopping was brought about by hydraulically assisted drum brakes all round.

The plastic upholstered interior could swallow four people and some luggage in a recess behind the rear seat and over the engine. Entry to the rear was by a single rear-hinged door mounted on the right-hand side of the car, good for European passengers alighting on the kerb side. Some cars were sold in the UK, but the door arrangement stayed as it was.

For use as a miniature van, the rear-seat back could be folded down for extra capacity. The conventional rear axle now fitted introduced semi-trailing independent rear suspension that made many more appearances over the following years for BMW passenger cars, except for the M1.

Production was stopped in December of 1959 to make way for the new more conventional-looking 700 series. Money was still an issue as motorcycle sales had continued to decline, with the German public demanding a conventional car rather than a motorcycle and sidecar. The 501s were way too big and expensive for the mass market, and the buying public were slowly turning to the new Volkswagen Beetle and other new offerings from Opel and Ford Germany.

The 600 was only road tested by the mainstream media in the UK in late 1958, when *Motor* magazine reported on the car that sat firmly between microcars and conventional saloons: "In Britain, perhaps, the greatest importance of the BMW 600 is, as a reminder to both manufacturers and buyers that, somewhere midway between these sizes, a compromise can be struck which combines most of the carrying capacity and effortless performance of one with most of the compactness and economy operation of the other."

There was still not yet a mid-size mass market saloon. The Neue Klasse saloons and coupés would fill this gap from 1963 after the company shareholders put forward a much needed major development plan in late 1959.

600 advertising slogans

BMW opens new doors to space and economy (600, 1959 USA)

Fur die Zukunft geschaffen (created for the future)

Das neue Profil' (The new profile)

The 600 somewhere in the Alps.

600 BODY TYPES: Two-door (one front hinging, one side hinging). **Manufactured at:** Munich. **Number produced:** 34,813, all left-hand drive. **Production span:** 1957-1959.
PERFORMANCE: **Top speed:** 64mph/110km/h; **0-50mph/85km/h:** 24.8 seconds; **average economy:** 50mpg.
PRICE AT LAUNCH: £676 or 3985 DM.
MEASUREMENTS: **Length:** 9ft 6in (2.9m); **height:** 4ft 6½in (1.38m); **width:** 4ft 7in (1.4m); **wheelbase:** 5ft 7in (1.71m); **kerb weight:** 1235lb (560kg); **wheels:** 10in; **turning circle:** 27ft (8.23m); **fuel capacity:** 5 gallons/22.5 litres; **boot capacity:** unquoted, but the rear seat backrest can fold down flat.
TECHNICAL: **Engine types:** 585cc two-cylinder air-cooled petrol; **gearbox:** four-speed manual (no automatic); **suspension:** Dubonnet independent with coil (front), independent trailing links and coil (rear); **brakes:** hydraulic drum front and rear.
TRIM: Plastic.
KEY OPTIONAL EXTRAS: Two-tone paintwork, fog lights.

The new 700 saloon on the production line.

An early production coupé with whitewall tyres.

700

The BMW 700 was the first car of unitary construction that the company built. Again, designer Willy Black continued the new 700 as a natural progression of his 600, by stretching the chassis and again using an off the shelf motorcycle power unit, again mounted at the rear. The R67 engine was 697cc and provided all the power the new project needed.

The final detail styling was by Michelotti, which was also responsible for the Triumph Herald and later DAF and front-wheel drive Triumph cars of the same period, and there are certainly similarities.

Michelotti proposed two ideas, one with a slanted roof (a coupé), and the other a standard two-door saloon, and a delighted BMW signed off both designs, which were identical from the waist down. The 700 was a sales success, with over 183,000 examples sold in its six-year production run.

Above: An early marketing photograph of the standard-length saloon.

Left: The front aspect of the 700.

The first model to be marketed was the two-plus-two coupé from June 1959, followed by the two-door saloon later in the year. Baur was commissioned to produce a fabric-roofed cabriolet version, and 2592 were built. This cabriolet looked stunning with the roof down but, when it was up, there was even less room in the rear than the standard coupé. The 700 coupé styling also bore a striking resemblance to the NSU Sport Prinz, which it was pitched against in magazine twin tests in the early 1960s.

When the range was available in the UK from late 1961, the price list was:

700 saloon	£893 18s
700 coupé	£1039 14s
700 cabriolet	£1249 4s

A competition roadster was also offered between 1961 and 1963, but only 19 examples were produced.

Despite its parentage, the 700 appeared wholly different to its Isetta and 600 forerunners, with proper boot space up front. Due to insufficient factory space – with Isettas and the big saloons being manufactured – the completed 700 bodies were provided by an outside supplier and delivered to Munich.

The 700 was powered by a 30hp version of the 697cc twin-cylinder engine, and this was upgraded to 40hp in 1960, and the Sport version featured a 9.0:1 compression ratio and twin carburation, complete with

Open air motoring in the mountains with the BMW 700 cabriolet.

twin rear anti-roll bars. An upmarket Luxus version appeared in 1961 with a 6in extension to the wheelbase, and a rebadge occurred a year later when the LS designation appeared. A very scarce longer wheelbase coupé was offered in 1964, of which only 1730 were built.

Overall, the 700 coupé performed well, appearing in several European rallies, including the Monte Carlo and the six-hour Nürburgring event.

The UK's *Motor* magazine tested a saloon at the tail end of 1961 and concluded, "Apart from attractive appearance and good finish, its main virtues are a high cruising speed, above average acceleration through the gears, and comfortable suspension."

The 700 series ended production in 1965. It had seen the company successfully through its financial turmoil. High hopes, for BMW as a company, were pinned on the Neue Klasse cars that had started appearing in 1963, initially as the 1500 four-door saloon, and then on profitable large-scale production.

700 BODY TYPES: Two-door saloon, coupé plus cabriolet. Some longer cars.
Manufactured at: Munich (final assembly) except cabriolet built in Stuttgart by Baur, and CKD form in Belgium, Italy, Argentina and Israel.
Number produced: 188,121.
Production span: 1959-1965.
PERFORMANCE: Top speed: 75-85mph/125-140km/h; **0-60mph/100km/h:** 29 seconds; **average economy:** 35-40mpg.
PRICE AT LAUNCH: £893 (UK in 1961; saloon price).
MEASUREMENTS: Length: 11ft 7¼in (3.54m) (from 1962 some models 12½in (0.3m) longer); **height:** coupé 4ft 2in (1.27m); saloon 4ft 5in (1.35m); **width:** 4ft 10in (1.47m); **wheelbase:** 6ft 11½in (2.13m)/7ft 6in (2.28m); **kerb weight:** 12¼ cwt (622kg); **wheels:** 12in; **turning circle:** 32ft 6in (9.9m); **fuel capacity:** 6 gallons/27 litres plus 1 gallon reserve; **boot capacity:** adequate for two suitcases; space shared up front with spare wheel.
TECHNICAL: Engine types: 697cc two-cylinder petrol; **gearbox:** four-speed manual; **suspension:** Dubonnet independent with coils (front), independent with single trailing wishbones and coils (rear); **brakes:** ATE hydraulic drums front and rear.
TRIM: plastic and fabric.
KEY OPTIONAL EXTRAS: Radio, fog lights.

700 advertising slogans
Graduate to a BMW
BMW 700 comes to Britain
Rush hour zip, highway zoom...
How to assemble a Saturday in spring
That's the car for me
Outstanding performance and economy with extra room and luxury seating (700 LS)
Judged by how it's made... and how many!
Impressive performance, comfort and economy (sports coupé)
Coming in the spring (convertible, 1962 advert from Canada)

NEW CLASS FROM 1962

The New Class or 'Neue Klasse' range of mid-size cars was the result of huge investment by BMW in the late 1950s and early 1960s. The existing motorcycle market was certainly diminishing, and the market demand had generally shifted up from small microcars and even the small 700, the public looking for a larger form of travel, with four-door cars in more demand, too. The big four-door 501 and 502 cars had been around for nearly a decade in various forms, and were still priced at the top end of the market.

For public assessment, BMW displayed a very early production 1500 saloon at the Frankfurt Motor Show in September 1961. On display was a brand-new monocoque-bodied car with mid-size new engine and 8ft 4½in wheelbase. It was the forerunner of several models to be used on that platform between a production start in 1962 to its final demise in 1972 with a best sales year of 1965. Its styling came from an in-house team helped by consultations with Michelotti in Italy.

1500 & 1600

The first and entry-level model of the range came in the form of the 1500 saloon, which was to be produced for two years until 1964, although some markets still took delivery of this model due to advantages on their new car taxation rules. Press reviews were favourable, commenting on its lively performance, excellent interior and luggage room and good driving characteristics with increased visibility. The 1500 retailed in the UK at a price of £1376, twice as much as its stablemate the 700. To put this into context, it was more expensive than any Ford on the price lists and the same price as the cheapest Jaguar, the 2.4 Mk2 (£1348). Acceleration is somewhat modest by today's standards (0-60mph in around 15 seconds) and top speed was a commendable 95mph. In all, 23,807 were manufactured in the same four-door shell.

A rare 1600 GT convertible, as restored by BMW apprentices by 2018.

Available from 1964, the 1600 directly replaced the 1500 except in certain markets. It had a 1573cc engine based on the M10 unit with the same bore as the new 1800 (see below) but with the stroke of the 1500. It lasted until early 1967 after 9728 units were made, all based on the same monocoque shell again, but was not listed on the UK price lists, where the 1500 soldiered on. Note this model name should not be confused with the 1600-2 launched around the same time as the original 1600's demise and covered in a later section of this book.

1800

Production was certainly ramped up for the New Class 1800, available from 1963 with a larger 90hp engine with displacement of 1773cc. Contemporary road testers favoured the spaciousness of the five-seater, the particularly good roadholding, tremendous solidity and well-insulated interior.

Tuner Alpina also joined the scene with its 1800 ti (Turismo Internazionale), which boasted dual Solex PHH two-barrel sidedraught carburettors and higher compression pistons good for 110hp. A front anti-roll bar was added to the specification, all for an extra £1500 on the list price.

The following year, the 1800 TI/SA (Sonderausfuhrung/special version) was a homologation special with dual Weber two-barrel carburettors and uprated brake discs. Sold only to approved racing drivers, 200 were built, each with anti-roll bars at the rear, and five-speed Getrag manual gearbox. Three-speed automatic transmission came as an option for the 1966 model year and cost an extra £150. Production continued largely

The New World 1800 in 1963. BMW really cranked up the production numbers of this model.

Top: The front aspect of the 2000 ti in 1966, and above, the rear aspect of the 2000 ti Lux.

unchanged until late 1968, when the 1800 was revised alongside the 2000 (see below), with changes including a revised heater, more up-to-date dashboard and detail changes to the front grille. Engine bore changes resulted in a new displacement of 1766cc. The last of any modifications to the eight-year-old 1800 were made towards the end of production in 1971, when the model received the same rectangular headlamps as the 2000, and wider tail lights. Nearly 161,000 of the 1800s were produced.

2000

Still within the same shell, the 110mph BMW 2000 four-door saloon was launched in 1966 with the following price structure:

2000 £1778
2000 auto £1927
2000 ti £1830
2000 ti Lux £1898

Identified by unique rectangular headlamps and wider tail lights, the 2000 range had extra chrome trim. As with many European imports, US models were fitted with round headlamps due to new regulations there. These saloons used the same engines from the coupé models (see below) with the ti derivative having twin Solex two-barrel sidedraught carburettors and a creditable 121hp, some 20hp extra. Wider wheels and tyres were fitted, plus front and rear anti-roll bars to the ti version. A more luxurious 2000 ti Lux soon joined the range with extra interior appointments including a wooden dashboard and (sometimes seen) optional leather seats. The 1800 improvements mentioned above for the 1800 cars were adopted for the 1969 model year including dual-circuit braking and new front grille. A 130hp 'Touring International Injected' 2000 tii boasted Kugelfischer mechanical fuel injection from 1969, a first for BMW, but sadly it did not make its way onto UK price lists. However, the Frazer Nash version was offered at £1941.

1500, 1600, 1800 AND 2000 BODY TYPE: Four-door saloon. **Manufactured at:** Munich. **Number produced:** 220,350. **Production span:** 1962-1972.
PERFORMANCE: Top speed: 95-114mph/150-185km/h
0-60mph/100km/h: 9.8-15 seconds; **average economy:** 26mpg.
PRICE AT LAUNCH: £1376 (1500).
MEASUREMENTS: Length: 14ft 9¼in (4.51m); **height:** 4ft 9in (1.44m); **width:** 5ft

The distinctive front lamps of the New World saloon series.

7in (1.71m); **wheelbase:** 8ft 4½in (2.55m); **kerb weight (1500/1600):** 2337lb (1060kg); **wheels:** 14in; **turning circle:** 31ft 5in (9.57m); **fuel capacity:** 11.7 gallons/53 litres; **boot capacity:** 13ft³.

TECHNICAL: **Engine types:** 1499, 1573, 1773, 1766, and 1990cc four-cylinder petrol; **gearbox:** four-speed manual and three-speed automatic; **suspension:** independent lower wishbone and MacPherson strut (front), independent semi trailing arms with coil (rear); **brakes:** disc front and either drum or disc rear.

TRIM: Double stretch leatherette.

KEY OPTIONAL EXTRAS: Transmission tunnel tray.

New Class saloons advertising slogans

Graduate to a BMW (1500)
New Class 1800/2000
It's no ordinary man who drives a BMW, it's no ordinary car either (1800/2000)
A symbol of engineering integrity (1800)
Good appearance, impressive performance, outstanding handling (1800 ti)
Unbeatable BMW! (1800 ti)
The 107mph quality-built family sports saloon (1800 ti)
The new high style competitor BMW (1800)
A BMW's best showroom is the open road! (1800)
Arrive with a BMW (1800)
Can a man fall in love with his car? (1800)
Record breaking. Brilliant Styling. The new BMW (1800, USA)
Family. Sport. Professional (1800 ti)
Switch on... the going is fast (two-litre sports saloon)
The new 2000 ti – another unbeatable BMW (1966)

The 2000 coupé

Karmann was responsible for the manufacture of the attractive new coupé version of the New Class cars from mid-1965 and up to 1969 at its Rheine facility after the demise of the V8 3200 CS. They bore, at least from the waist up, a striking resemblance to the later 1968-1975 E9 cars and were marketed as 2000 C (single carburettor and 100hp fitted initially with a three-speed automatic gearbox then, from 1967, a manual) and 115mph 2000 CS (twin carburettor and 120hp fitted with a four-speed manual gearbox). Over and above the 2000 saloons, they had a new front end and sat about 4in lower. An unusual approach was that of painted body colour between the grille

The front of the 2000ti with grille badge.

In the 1970s, the trim piece was altered across the leading edge of the bonnet.

The dashboard arrangement of the 2000 ti Lux.

and under the headlamps, which is surely an acquired taste, but did set out to identify the marque when it was closing in on the rear-view mirror. The American market had this arrangement too, but again with twin round headlamps on each side.

The retail prices and production numbers of the New Series coupés were:

2000 CS: £2950 (9999 produced)
2000 C auto: £2950 (3249 produced)
2000 C manual: (£ not quoted) (443 produced)

The coupé was a very rare sight in the UK, and was superseded by the impressively

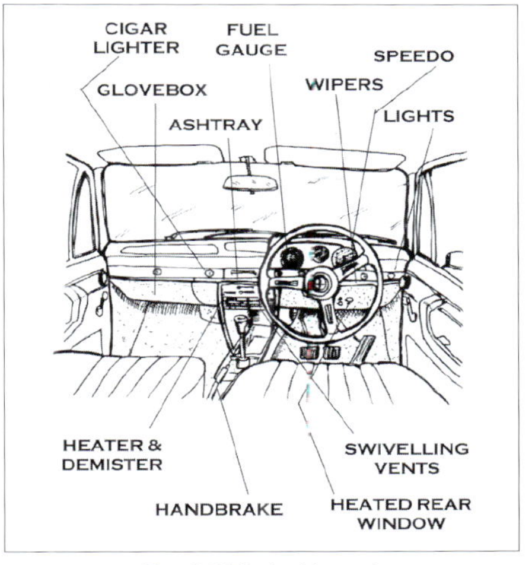

The 2000 dashboard.

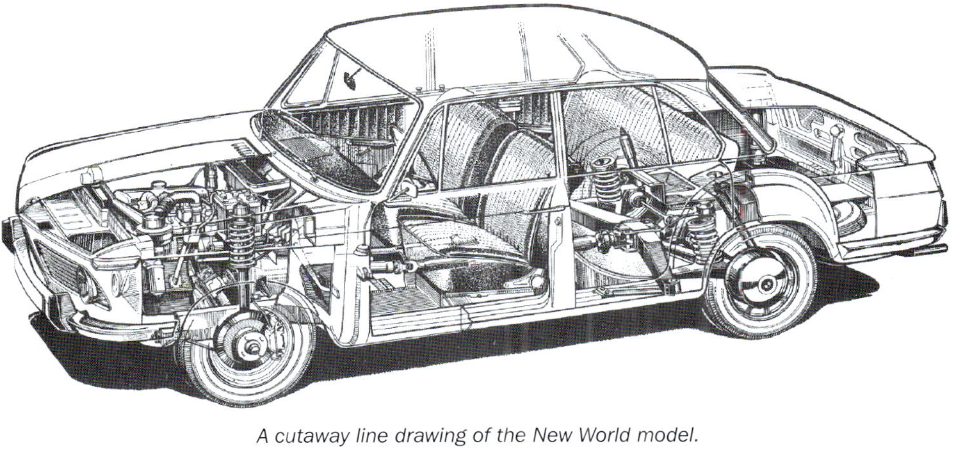

A cutaway line drawing of the New World model.

refreshed E9 coupés from 1968 until 1975, which paved the way for the new 6 Series.

2000 C/ CS BODY TYPE: Two-door coupé. **Manufactured at:** Rheine. Numbers produced: 2837 C and 8883 CS. **Production span:** 1965-1968.
PERFORMANCE: Top speed (CS): 115mph/180km/h; **0-60mph/100km/h (CS):** 10.5 seconds; **average economy:** 18-24mpg.
PRICE AT LAUNCH: £2950 for either model.
MEASUREMENTS: Length: 14ft 10¼in (4.53m); **height:** 4ft 5½in (1.36m); **width:** 5ft 5½in (1.67m); **wheelbase:** 8ft 4½in (2.55m); **kerb weight:** 2650lb (1202kg); **wheels:** 14in; **turning circle:** 32ft 0in (9.75m); **fuel capacity:** 11.7 gallons/53 litres; **boot capacity:** 13ft³.
TECHNICAL: Engine types: 1990cc four-cylinder petrol; **gearbox:** four-speed manual or three-speed automatic; **suspension:** independent lower wishbone and MacPherson strut (front), independent semi trailing arms with coil (rear); **brakes:** front disc rear drum.
TRIM: Double stretch leatherette.

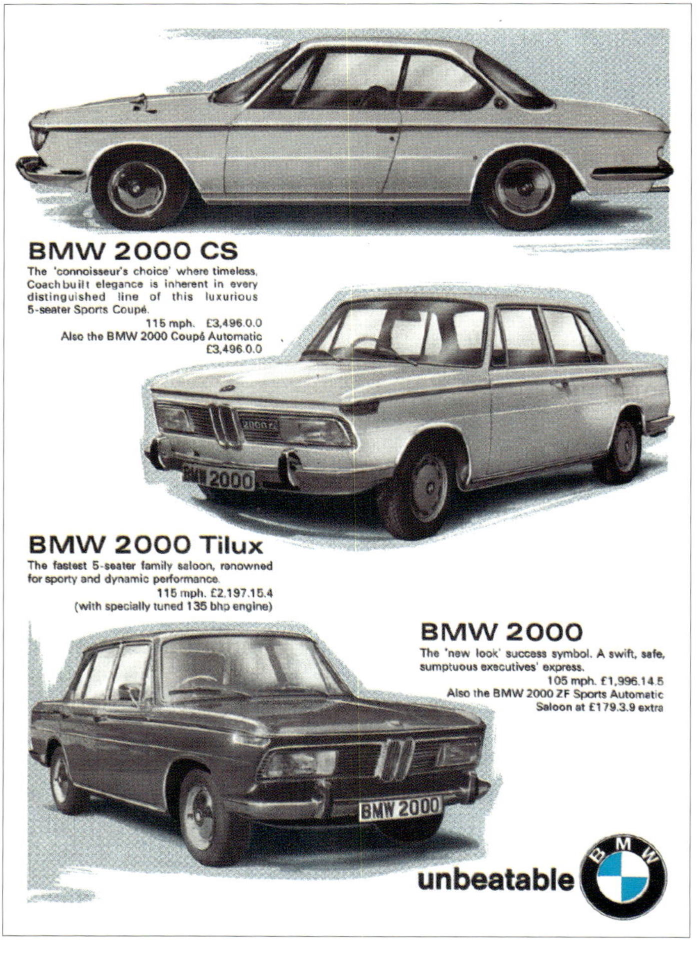

The 2000 CS coupé shown at the top of this UK advertisement, dubbed "the connoisseur's choice."

1966-1977 – 02 SERIES

The 02 range of compact BMW cars was produced between March 1966 and summer 1975, with production and marketing immediately slotting in directly behind the 700 saloons of the early 1960s. In Germany the 02 model range was known as the Flustern Bombe (whispering bomb). It was launched outside Munich Opera House to coincide with the firm's 50th anniversary. Four two-door body styles were utilised across the range, a three-box style saloon often referred to as the coupé due to poor rear legroom, an estate marketed as the Touring from early 1971 to 1974, a targa-top open car plus a more traditional fabric-roofed cabriolet style produced by Baur on the same 8ft 2½in wheelbase.

Not all 02-specific models used each of these body styles, as described below. All the 02s were petrol engine four-cylinders and, mechanically, the range was identical across each of the body styles. Much advertising marketing was evident in Europe and in America, initially in black and white form, then full colour by the early 1970s. As always, a non-exhaustive list of the media advertising slogans is reproduced after each section, with translations into English given where necessary. With the inception of the earliest-generation E21 3 Series in July 1975, the 02s were slowly phased out, with the 1502 economy version making a two-year appearance, with availability lasting until 1977. Notably, the touring version seemed less popular, with sales increasing as the model continued; its 30-degree straight tailgate line offering extra cubic capacity for weekend-away holdalls and golf clubs.

Slightly smaller than the 2000 range, the 2002 was marketed as a coupé, and was always offered on a two-door platform.

1600-2 & 1602

The 1600-2 was the first of the 02 BMWs to make an appearance in 1966. The unusual name was derived as this was, effectively, the second type of 1600. The previous four-door 1600 (based on the 1800) used the name first, so a distinction had to be made to avoid any confusion. Allowing for relevant car

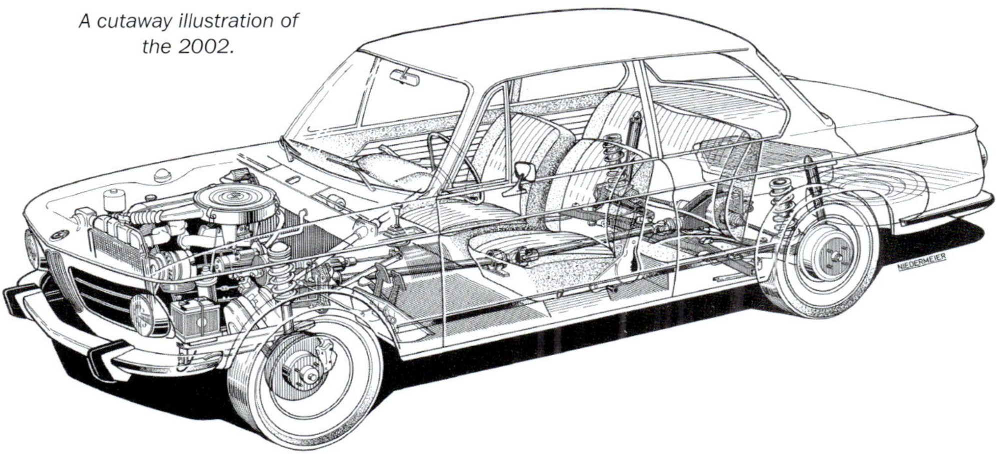

A cutaway illustration of the 2002.

An unknown desert location makes the perfect backdrop for this posed publicity photo.

taxes, costing a shade under £1300, make no mistake, this was no economy priced car, costing over double the price of a standard £600 Mini Cooper of the day, and even more than an Austin-Healey 3000 (£1126). In fact, its price almost mirrored the TVR Mk3 1800 S (£1221).

The saloon bodywork was an attractive package and sat on a MacPherson strut front end and semi-trailing rear suspension. A Michelotti-styled touring version followed in 1968, effectively a three-door hatchback, as did the Baur convertible, but these rarely saw markets outside Germany and are quite collectable today. A single-carburettor 1600-2 model initially started the range, followed by a twin Solex BHH carburettor 1600 ti model in September 1967, where the ti stands for 'Touring International'. The latter, which was never officially imported to the UK, was dropped a year later to make way for the single-carburettor 2002. In the US, the 1600 ti could not be imported, as the federal smog device would not work on the multi-carburettor engine, but more on that later with the 2002 …

UK's *Motor* weekly magazine

US-bound models were identified by an extra reflector just under the indicator light on the front wing.

A UK advertisement for the model range, headed by the 2002 in the 1960s.

More of the UK model range in the mid-1960s.

The later 02 Touring model was effectively a three-door hatchback. This is the 1802.

The round rear lamps of the Touring. This is the 2000.

got its hands on a 1969 1600 saloon example and it formed part of its sports car group test in an October 1969 edition against strong competition: the Ford Capri 2000GT, the Fiat 124 Sport Coupé, the Bond Equipe 2-litre GT and the new fastback Sunbeam Rapier from Rootes. Performance and economy were largely mid-range for the BMW, but its handling was a firm favourite. The magazine concluded that the Fiat seemed to be the best car overall, including its good looks, but said of the 1600, "The large boot of the BMW gives it a little more appeal to the man with a large family, although it is as sporting a car as any and possibly the fastest through the corners."

Alpina produced, at the time, an ultimate Q car; its 1600 Alpina model fitted with the new 2-litre seen in the larger saloons – and five-speed gearbox – and this model was also available for export.

American magazine *Road & Track* tested a rare US example in 1967 and a staff member remarked about the $5579 price tag that included all the extra taxation required to get it into the country, "Holy Deutch-marks, you could almost buy a Porsche 911 for that kind of bread!" A double-size fuel tank (20 US gallons) was fitted to the test car, and performance was superb, with a top speed of 125mph and a 0-60mph acceleration time of 8.3 seconds. Extra heavy-duty suspension, adjustable Koni shock absorbers and anti-sway bars were fitted, and extra instrumentation included a tachometer in place of the clock, the larger engine having a red line of 7200rpm. The look was completed internally by special Recaro bucket seats up front. The magazine concluded about the handling: "We have seldom driven a car which is as confidence-inspiring on twisting roads." Modest badging was kept to the standard 1600 motif on the boot panel, while chrome Alpina badges were fitted to the top of the front wings.

In very early 1971, the model was rebranded the 1602, by which time over 144,000 normally aspirated cars had been produced and 10,836 ti models. Wraparound bumpers followed across the entire 02 range in April 1971 and the 1602 soldiered on as basically a cheaper version of the 2002 until 1975 – by which time another 135,000 had been built – when it was replaced by the more economical 1502 run-out model described later in this section. A 1602 Touring was not generally available in the UK.

Two unusual

A 2000 Touring with the later black front grille.

concept cars were used for the 1972 Olympics in Munich: the 1602e Elektras. These saloons were fitted with a 772lb (350kg) pack of 12 lead acid batteries installed under the bonnet, and had a limited 20-mile range. For publicity, they were used to transport the long-distance walkers and provide backup for the marathon runners. From 1973 a significant styling update occurred across the 02 range; modifications included the adoption of black plastic grilles that made the cars look wider, oblong rear lamps on all saloons and convertibles, the touring version retaining the existing round-style units. There was a refreshed interior too, with a more modern four-spoke steering wheel and upgraded trim and interior appointments. A Lux option was now introduced with upgraded carpets, seat and facia trim, and the adoption of rear safety belts. This lasted until 1975 and retailed at just under £2500 when deleted.

The (1600) convertible boasted a soft top that laid completely flat when lowered.

1600-2, 1602 BODY TYPES: Two-door coupé, targa top and convertible. **Manufactured at:** Munich. **Number produced:** 252;282 1600-2; 10;836 1600 ti and 1255 1600 GT. **Production span:** 1966-1972.
PERFORMANCE (1602 SPECIAL): **Top speed:** 100mph/160km/h; **0-60mph/100km/h:** 11.9 seconds; **average economy:** 30mpg.
MEASUREMENTS: **Length:** 13ft 10½in (4.23m); **height:** 4ft 7½in (1.41m); **width:** 6ft 2in (1.88m); **wheelbase:** 7ft ½in (2.15m); **kerb weight:** 2160lb (980kg); **wheels:** 13in; **turning circle:** 30ft 0in (9.14m); **fuel capacity:** 10 gallons/45.4 litres; **boot capacity:** 10.8ft³.
TECHNICAL: **Engine type:** 1573cc four-cylinder petrol; **gearbox:** four-speed manual; **suspension:** independent with anti-roll bar, MacPherson strut (front), independent with semi-trailing arm; coil springs (rear); **brakes:** disc front drum rear.
TRIM: Vinyl or cloth.

1600, 1602 & 1802 advertising slogans
Successful men choose BMW (1600 coupé)
The 5 seater family coupe (1600 coupé)
Internationally acclaimed (1600 coupé)
Das Auto de Jahre (1974 1602)/The Car of the Year
Gruppen-Dynamik (1974 1602)/Group Dynamics
Wo sich die Geister sheiden (1974 1602)/ Where spirits meet
Der Zweck heiligt die Mitte (1974 1602)/The End Justifies the Centre
Wo sich die Geister scheiden. (1974 1602/2002 tii)/Where opinions differ

The Baur convertible had the benefit of a hard top.

2002

Following cries from American 1602 importers for a more powerful model, and noting that the 1602 tii did not meet local emission controls, the 2002 model was introduced in 1968 across the globe and to a 180-strong UK dealership base (deliveries from early 1970 in the UK, although some early models crept through) and lasted until 1975, when the new 3 Series replaced it. The 2002 had a higher drive ratio than the 1602, which gave it longer legs for touring. It was offered in touring bodywork when that arrived in the early 1970s, cabriolet (or targa-type) convertibles and the standard three-door saloon.

Just to confuse matters, the touring version was originally badged as a 2000! Seating was by way of Ambla PVC material, a little austere to some tastes. The 2002 was easily identified from its earlier lesser 1600 stablemates by a blackened front grille – but retained the chrome outlines. Power came from the existing 1990cc four-cylinder engine. In 1971, a 2002 tii was introduced, with a confusing-looking boot badge, but the acronym is explained thus: Touring International Injection. Fuel injection came from Kugelfischer, and these faster long-distance sprinter models featured revised synchromesh gearing, stiffer bodywork and dampers,

The later dashboard, this one from the tourer.

The earlier round rear lamps of the 02 range.

The trim on the Elektra prototype version was quite sumptuous.

Left: Later 02s had the squarer rear lamps, seen here on a 1975-6 UK model. Right: the door handle of the same model, and below: the interior of the same right-hand drive car.

uprated tyres with 5J rims and an additional £400 price loading over the standard 2002, and 30hp.

Road testers of the day often remarked about the pillarless door windows introducing extra wind noise above 80mph but, as always, they loved the impressive handling. The head office advertising copywriters were soon to jump on board with the prowess the new model possessed. "From out of nowhere, a spec appears in your rear view mirror, grows instantly larger, and you see the framed blue and white medallion on the bonnet. That's the brilliant new BMW 2002 bearing down on you ... BMW one schnell of a car!" Catapult-like acceleration was mentioned with "a breath taking" 0-50mph in 6.8 seconds. An automatic version was available in the UK from autumn 1969, the UK Targa appeared in February 1973 and, along with the 1602, the front grilles went entirely black from September of 1973 with the larger squared-out rear lamps arriving at the same time again, except for the touring versions. These hatchback cars were not as popular with the German market as had been hoped for, with some news stories of the larger body not being as stable as the saloon on the high-speed autobahns.

In 1974, some celebrity racing drivers – including Tony Bancroft, Gerry Marshall, Tony Lanfranchi and TV comedy actor from *Bless This House* Robin Stewart – took a fleet of new 2002s from Leeds to London on an extended economy run. Over £2500 was raised for British Epilepsy funds, with the winning car of Tony Lanfranchi achieving an astonishing 47.88mpg. Graham Ashley-Smith, in the Whitbread-sponsored car, commented in jest that there must have been a hole in the fuel tank, as it only achieved 26.66mpg. All cars had their fuel tanks sealed at the start and additional fuel carefully measured in at the end at the Slough finish.

2002 special editions

The 2002 GT4 was a Frua-designed fastback coupé model, where just two were produced and publicly displayed at coachwork shows in 1968 and 1969. A limited edition 2002 ti Diana was also later sold on the continent to celebrate the marriage of racer Hubert Hahne to Diana Koerner. It featured a leather interior and Italian alloy wheels.

Production of the touring body stopped in 1974, and the 2002 was phased out with the advent of the E21 3 Series in July 1975.

A German 02 model range press advert.

To bring the bumper heights in line with new American safety standards, post-1974 models had their heights raised by placing spacers over the top of the MacPherson struts.

The price list was as follows at its demise:

2002	£2946
2002 (auto)	£3194
2002 Lux	£3038
2002 Lux (auto)	£3346
2002 tii	£3499
2002 tii Lux	£3649
2002 cabriolet	£3877

2002 BODY TYPES: Two-door coupé, targa top and convertible plus touring from 1971. **Manufactured at:** Munich. **Number produced:** 330,035 2002 plus 16,488 2002 ti and 38,703 tii. **Production span:** 1968-1975.
PERFORMANCE (2002 tii): Top speed: 120mph/193km/h; **0-60mph/100km/h:** 8.2 seconds; **average economy:** 24mpg.
PRICE AT LAUNCH: £2299 (tii).
MEASUREMENTS: Length: 13ft 10½in (4.23m); **height:** 4ft 7½in (1.41m); **width:** 6ft 2in (1.88m); **wheelbase:** 7ft ½in (2.15m); **kerb weight:** 2160lb (980kg); **wheels:** 13in; **turning circle:** 30ft 0in (9.14m); **fuel capacity:** 10 gallons/45.4 litres; **boot capacity:** 10.8ft^3.
TECHNICAL: Engine type: 1990cc four-cylinder petrol; **gearbox:** four-speed manual; **suspension:** independent with anti-roll bar, MacPherson strut (front), independent with semi-trailing arm, coil springs (rear); **brakes:** disc front drum rear.
TRIM: Skai.

2002 advertising slogans

Move over... (1968)
BMW goes like schnell, move over...
Some BMW test drives are more demanding than others (RAC Rally) 2002 tii
Jekyll and Hyde
The sports cars in saloon clothing
Even with 106mph top, a few extra inches makes all the difference (Touring)
Good news travels fast
How to get ahead
For 5 years straight, the readers of Car & Driver have voted BMW the world's best sports sedan
Fast poke (1973)
BMW comes from a tough neighbourhood
The worst road you can find is the best place to find out about BMW|
2002. Love of a Lifetime
The giant-killer
Why BMW owners are fanatics
The BMW 2002 tii. It'll really move you
Innere Furrung/Internal Furring
The BMW 2002 is practical, roomy and economical. But in spite of all that it isn't boring.
Can a man fall in love with his car?
In Germany they say Bey Em Vey. And they get out of the way
You're not really going to try to pass this BMW are you?
Richtungs-Anzeige/Direction Indicator
If you know about BMW, you either own one or want one

2002 Turbo

With a bodyshell already six years old, BMW adopted the 02 shell for its new homologation racing 2002 Turbo in 1974. To qualify for Group 1 racing to the FIA, a certain number

of identical cars have to be built, to ensure that racing drivers are actually entering 'true production saloons'. Less than the obligatory 5000 cars were produced (figures largely state 1672 were manufactured), so the new model settled for Group 2 racing, with less than 200 entering the UK in 1974 and 1975, all in left-hand drive form, as it was all but impossible to revise the steering for right-hand drive. BMW had already won the Group 5 European Touring Car Championship in a 205hp turbocharged version of the 2002 in 1969, fitted with long-range fuel tank and Plexiglass plastic side windows.

Outwardly, the 2002 Turbo (2002 TIK) really made a visual statement. While the 2002 shell was recognised instantly, there were extra wide bolt-on-style wheelarches, deep-dish front air dam spoiler replacing the front bumper, vivid BMW Motor Sports graphics, extra-wide exhaust pipe, with the larger rear lamp clusters now available on the model range and a bold turbo emblem on the left side of the rear. A larger-than-average spoiler was added to the boot lid, and the Mahle wheels fitted were unique to the turbo model. Front and rear screens used all-black rubber, unlike their slower cousins that always saw some chrome striping within the surround. Inside had revised instrumentation, headrests, Rentrop-style rally seats and an all-important turbo boost gauge. Technical changes were a strengthened gearbox, limited-slip differential, revised spring and damper rates, wider 5.5J wheels, and the turbo unit was an off-the-shelf KKK unit. Performance was stunning, with a 0-60mph of about 6.6 seconds, with the tail sliding out happily on wet city streets. Track top speed was a commendable 128mph, but the German road safety lobby was quick to ask the factory to remove the reversed turbo (O-B-R-U-T) decal from the front spoiler, as it was deemed too provocative.

When deleted at the end of 02 production, the turbo model cost £4221 in the UK. As a homage to the 2002 Turbo, BMW produced a pair of concept cars: the 2002 Hommage Concept and the 2002 Hommage Turbomeister Concept in 2015.

Broadspeed was famous in the UK for producing tidy conversion turbo versions of many existing production cars and had already produced the 2002 Turbo Bullit. This special bespoke model had a top speed of 138mph and similar acceleration figures to the factory versions.

A German 2002 Turbo press advert. By now, the reversed TURBO badges on the lower spoiler were no longer fitted.

2002 TURBO BODY TYPES: Two-door coupé. **Manufactured at:** Munich. **Number produced:** 1672 (51 came to UK, all left-hand drive). **Production span:** 1973-1974.
PERFORMANCE: Top speed: 130mph/km/h, **0-60mph/100km/h:** 7.9 seconds; **average economy:** 25mpg.
MEASUREMENTS: Length: 13ft 10½in (4.23m); **height:** 4ft 7½in (1.41m); **width:** 6ft 2in (1.88m); **wheelbase:** 7ft ½in (2.15m); **kerb weight:** 2160lb (980kg); **wheels:** 13in; **turning circle:** 30ft 0in (9.15m); **fuel capacity:** 10 gallons/45.4 litres; **boot capacity:** 10.8ft³.
TECHNICAL: Engine types: 1990cc four-cylinder petrol; **gearbox:** four-speed manual; **suspension:** independent with anti-roll bar, MacPherson strut (front), independent with semi-trailing arm, coil springs (rear); **brakes:** disc front drum rear.
TRIM: Cloth.

The 2002 Turbo on the test track.

The interior of the 2002 Turbo.

2002 Turbo advertising slogans
Evolution (2002 Turbo)
Weil es sinn hat, hat es auch methode/ Because it has meaning it also has method

Later 1802 & 1502

Just 4075 1802 models were sold on the continent between launch in 1971 and the 1975 end date for the 1802 model, and it was never officially sold in the UK. This was a slightly cheaper model than the 2002, taking advantage of some company car tax breaks and available in two-door saloon and touring body formats. Over the four-year production period, 83,352 were sold.

A 1502 model was marketed between 1975 and 1977, another economy version of the now-deleted 1602, with 75bhp 1573cc engines replacing the previous 85bhp unit. The revised engine was tuned to run on lower-octane fuels after public demand for more economical cars due to the fuel crisis, with a new compression ratio of 8.0:1 with just 74hp, with 96mph still achievable. They were not available in the US and had some trim deleted to reduce production costs. Anti-roll bars were not fitted, and steel wheels replaced alloys and the interior featured just static safety belts for all passengers, while inertia reel leatherette trim were options. Not too many of these sold in the UK, as it never really had the marketing, with sales brochures depicting German cars and no press adverts. "The small step up to the 1502 is the great leap forward to BMW" stated the blurb at the start of the simple sales brochure, indicating it was deemed an entry-level car opening up the whole range for the future. It hardly set the world on fire with its performance (96mph/155km/h and 0-60mph in 13.8 seconds), with turbo diesel cars soon entering the market with much better performance figures. It ended home availability at £3118, some £800 cheaper than the base 316 model, which essentially replaced it when it was discontinued. Overall, the production figure was 71,976 units.

1802 AND 1502 BODY TYPES: Two-door coupé. **Manufactured at:** Munich. **Number produced:** 83,351 1802. **Production span:** 1971-1977.
PERFORMANCE (1602 SPECIAL):
Top speed: 100mph/160km/h;
0-60mph/100km/h: 11.9 seconds; **average economy:** 30mpg.
MEASUREMENTS: Length: 13ft 10½in (4.23m); **height:** 4ft 7½in (1.41m); **width:** 6ft 2in (1.88m); **wheelbase:** 7ft ½in (2.15m); **kerb weight:** 2160lb (980kg); **wheels:** 13in; **turning circle:** 30ft 0in (9.14m);

The rear aspect of the 2002 Turbo, this one from Nevada, US.

fuel capacity: 10 gallons/45.4 litres; **boot capacity:** 10.8ft³.
TECHNICAL: Engine type: 1573cc four-cylinder petrol; **gearbox:** four-speed manual; **suspension:** independent with anti-roll bar, MacPherson strut (front), independent with semi-trailing arm, coil springs (rear); **brakes:** disc front drum rear.
TRIM: Vinyl or cloth.

1502 advertising slogans

Der Blick nach vorn (1975 1502)/The look ahead

Nuova BMW 1502: continua il mito BMW (1975 1502)/New BMW 1502: the BMW myth continues

BMW – sheer driving pleasure

BMW 1502: Long-lasting driving pleasure

A 2002 Turbo cutaway engine illustration.

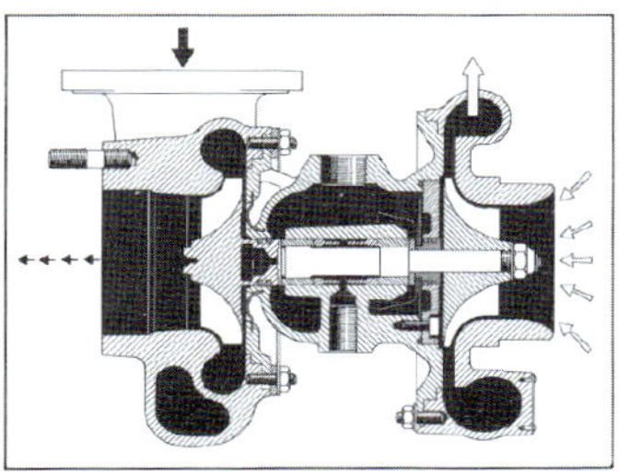

1968-1977 – 2500, 2800, 3.0 & 3.3 (E3 & E9)

A total nine-year production run of the larger 'New Six' cars started in 1968, with the E3 saloon (1968-1977) and the E9 coupés (1968-1975). After a five-year absence, the new models marked BMW's return to large, full-size luxury cars since the demise of the 501 and 502. The ageing V8s had been destined for the museum, but the New Six cars were built with a new M30 straight-six engine developed in the early to mid-1960s and based on the existing M10 four-cylinder units, a strong attempt to tackle Mercedes-Benz head-on in this lucrative market. Sharing this same engine, transmission and other key components, the E9 coupés were built on a shortened E3 saloon platform with design work for body E3 and E9 starting in 1965. Styling was in-house by Wilhelm Hofmeister, with finishing touches outsourced to Italian design houses Michelotti, again, and Bertone. The E3 and E9 range was successful, and over a quarter of a million were produced, the saloon selling around seven times faster than the coupé. Availability on overseas market started later in 1969.

Langley Motors in Thames Ditton, UK, was quick to jump on the estate car conversion market, and it produced an attractive and capacious shooting brake or, to use its future model designation, tourer.

E3 saloons

Initially, the 2.8-litre cars were marketed always as four-door vehicles, to be joined by the 3-litre in 1971, which was also offered in fuel-injected form. The 3-litre cars replaced the 2.8 on the UK price lists, while the 2500 continued until the end of E3 saloon production. For a couple of years a fuel-injected 3.3-litre version joined the range (1974-1976) with a special £8651 fully equipped stretched 3.3 Li version from 1976 to 1977 aimed more at the chauffer's market. The extra length was built into the wheelbase and rear doors.

A UK press advert for the E3 2500 and 2800 saloons.

The 3.3 Li came with an electrically operated sunroof, stereo radio cassette, white leather upholstery, headlamp washers, Borg Warner 65 automatic transmission and full air-conditioning. While no options were available in the UK for the right-hand drive model, in Germany the car could be ordered with wider wheels and tyres and a limited-slip differential. Its top rivals included the 450 SEL Mercedes, Jaguar XJ12, Iso Rivolta Fidia and even the ageing Rolls-Royce Silver Shadow. From 1976 on, L-Jetronic fuel injection replaced

the earlier D-Jetronic Bosch system on all top models. As a run-out model, some overseas markets saw the long-wheelbase body powered by the 2.8-litre engine, with 5036 versions sold in left-hand drive form only.

E3 BODY TYPES: Four-door saloon (estates by an outside converter). **Manufactured at:** Munich. **Number produced:** 220,957. **Production span:** 1968-1977.
PERFORMANCE (2500 AUTOMATIC): Top speed: 115mph/180km/h; **0-60mph/100km/h:** 11.9 seconds; **average economy:** 25mpg.
PRICE AT LAUNCH: £2958 (2.5); £3245 (2.8) from late 1969.
MEASUREMENTS: Length: 15ft 5in (4.7m) (3.3 Li is 5in

Left: "The 125mph dream car, for the man who can please himself." The 2800 shown on a UK press advertisement.

European Motor Show picture of the new, large saloons.

A very early production E3 saloon.

longer); **height:** 4ft 9in (1.45m); **width:** 6ft 5in (1.96m); **wheelbase:** 8ft 10in (2.7m), LWB is 9ft 2in (2.79m); **kerb weight:** 2968 (1346kg); **wheels:** 14in; **turning circle:** 30ft (9.14m); **fuel capacity:** 16.5 gallons/75 litres; **boot capacity:** 12.3ft³.
TECHNICAL: **Engine types:** 2494, 2788, 2985, 3295 and 3210cc six-cylinder petrol; **gearbox:** four-speed manual; or three-speed automatic; **suspension:** independent MacPherson struts with coil springs (front), independent with trailing arms and coil springs (rear); **brakes:** disc all round.
TRIM: Plastic, cloth and leather.
KEY OPTIONAL EXTRAS: Automatic transmission.

E3 advertising slogans
The 125mph car that money alone can't buy (2500/2800)
The 121mph executive express is now leaving Gerrards Cross (2500)
Inside every driver there's a BMW owner (2500)
The 125mph dream car for the man who can please himself (2500/2800)
"To me it's a high powered sports car… she still thinks it's a luxury saloon" (3.0 Si)
Why is the Bavarian Motor Works sending the 2500/2800 BMW's to America?
It takes one to catch one (3.0 Si)
All right George. I'll drive today (2500)
Inside every driver there's a BMW owner (2500)
The expert's choice (2500/2800)
Two in One (2500/2800)
Vive la difference (3.0S)
BMW active safety (2500)
The power behind the power (3.0L)
Take me to your husband (3.0S)
Hot Car from Bavaria (2800)
Be a sport (2800, 1970)
There is no substitute for breeding (3.0 LA, 1977)
This is one of the athletes you'll see at the 1972 Olympics (2800)
The man who buys the new £3,699 BMW 3.0S isn't flashing his wallet
The 132mph BMW 3.0 Si. When it's a matter of power
They'll miss you at the local (3.0 LA petrol station)
Efficiency expert (3.0, USA)
The fastest three-litre saloon on earth (3.0 Si)

E9 coupés

The E9 coupés were introduced at the same time as the E3 saloons. A key change compared with the predecessor New Class series was that this time the coupés, from the base of the windscreen down, were identical at the front top to the new saloons. Rival Opel had adopted this approach a decade later with the Senator saloon and Monza coupé, again built on the same platform. The bodywork was built by Karmann and should only be referred to

Left: The more powerful 3.0i saloon.
Below left: The interior of the rear that benefited from the extra wheelbase of the 3.3L.
Below: The 3.3L had a longer wheelbase.
Bottom right: The 3.3L automatic, rear aspect.

as a 2+2 configuration. The wheelbase of the coupé was around 3in shorter than the normal-wheelbase saloon - 7in shorter than the long-wheelbase saloons, and the coupé range was also available in the UK market, unlike the previous New Class coupés. *Motor* magazine road tested a 2800 CS with the manual four-speed ZF gearbox in 1971 and commented, "Make no mistake, we all enjoyed and admired this luxury driving machine. It handles quite well, has a nice gearbox, excellent seats, heating and ventilation; and is endowed with an undeniable inbuilt air of quality, pedigree and style."

The 3.0 Si could reach 131mph, as stated in this UK advertisement. This is a late model car with front bib spoiler.

Three-litre engines were added to the range in 1972 in normally aspirated form – the CS – and fuel injection too. The manual transmission-only 200hp 3.0 CSi was rapid (141mph and 0-60mph in 7.5 seconds) and both came with higher gearing and power steering as standard, as were two-speed wipers, hazard warning lights and a heated rear window. The £5828 CSI was identified only by a small 'i' designation on the boot panel.

The ultimate derivative of the E9 series was the charismatic CSL coupé, a homologation special produced between 1972 and 1975. Just over a thousand were produced initially with a 3003cc in-line six-cylinder engine, then a longer-stroke 3153cc version, built so the car could compete in a larger-capacity ETC racing class. Light alloy skin panels formed the bodywork, and a general weight reduction resulted in rather skimpy use of internal trim. Only 39 examples of the so called 'Batmobile' were built between 1973 and 1975, identified by a larger rear spoiler and other bespoke aerodynamic aids.

A press photo of the 3.0 CS coupé with fog lamps.

The E9 lasted until 1976,

when it was replaced by the similar-looking new E24 6 Series, when the E3 saloons soldiered on to be replaced a year later by the new 7 Series.

E9 BODY TYPES: Three-door coupé. **Manufactured at:** Munich. **Number produced:** 29,626. **Production span:** 1968-1975. **PERFORMANCE (2800 CS): Top speed:**

The E9 coupé had this BMW roundel at the base of the 'C' pillar.

Left: A Bavarian Cream advert for the 3.0 CS: "it may be the best car in the world".

Below: Ride fast. Ride free. Ride easy. The 132mph 3.0 sports coupé press advert.

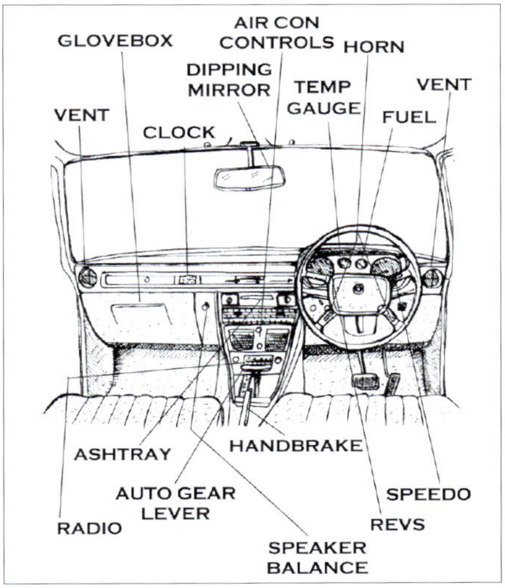

The 33L dashboard.

Left: The E9 coupé being track tested.

Below: Four shots of a pristine 3.0 CS survivor. Top left: As photographed in 2024. Top right and bottom left: The same car impresses the Suffolk crowds on the annual Ipswich to Felixstowe road run. The event attracts thousands, starting in Christchurch Park, Ipswich, and motoring through to Felixstowe promenade. Bottom right: The pristine headlamps are shown.

128mph/205km/h; **0-60mph/100km/h:** 8.5 seconds; **average economy:** 23mpg.
PRICE AT LAUNCH: £4996 (2800 in 1969).
MEASUREMENTS: Length: 15ft 3½in (4.66m); **height:** 4ft 6in (1.37m); **width:** 5ft 5½in (1.66m); **wheelbase:** 8ft 7in (2.62m); **kerb weight:** 26.8cwt (1361kg); **wheels:** 14in; **turning circle:** 29ft (8.84m); **fuel capacity:** 15.4 gallons/70 litres; **boot capacity:** approx. 10ft^3.
TECHNICAL: Engine types: 2494, 2788, 2986, 3003, 3153cc six-cylinder petrol; **gearbox:** four-speed manual or three-speed automatic; **suspension:** independent by inclined MacPherson struts, coil springs and anti-roll bar (front), independent by semi-trailing arm and coil springs with anti-roll bar (rear); **brakes:** front disc, rear drum, rear disc on 3-litre and CSL cars.
TRIM: Plastic or cloth.
KEY OPTIONAL EXTRAS: Automatic transmission.

E9 advertising slogans
The Exorcist (3.0 CSi)
BMW 1st in Group 2 Le Mans. Unbeatable (3.0 CSL)
Ride fast Ride free Ride easy, ride the new (3.0 CS)

1972-1988 – 5 SERIES (E12 & E28)

E12, the first 5 Series

The new 5 Series model range paved the way for the future of the BMW badging system. It had used the three-digit approach for a model name with a historical nod in the direction of the 320 in 1934 and the 500 series in the immediate post-war era. The new E12 5 Series was the first of eight 5 Series model ranges produced, as at the time of writing. The BMW four-cylinder three-box shape saloons had been successfully sold since the early 1960s, in the form of the 1800 and later 2000 models in a variety of models, but change came in the early 1970s.

An early brochure cover for the first-generation 5 Series.

The handsome new 5 Series saloon owed some of its exterior good looks to the 2002 ti styling exercise by Bertone in 1970. It was launched at the autumn Games of the XX Olympiad, the Olympics at Munich in 1972, at the purpose-built park very close to the BMW engine factory, but its launch was somewhat overshadowed by the infamous atrocities at the venue, and afterwards. The new five-seat 520 was of similar width and height to its predecessor, but was 5in longer, mainly due to a 3½in-longer wheelbase. Bodywork was clean, crisp and functional. The front grille and windscreen wipers were blackened like the contemporary 2002 models. The central rubber protection trim along the bodysides was lowered to match the height of the rubber-capped chrome bumpers, its length abbreviated by both wheelarches each side. The selling spearhead was essentially 'bigger inside but not outside', made possible by the

American press advertising for the 530i.

The rear aspect of the 520.

longer wheelbase that was now approaching the dimension of the bigger 2500 cars. That said, it gave greater rear legroom than the 1800 and 2300.

Production started in earnest in July of 1972 at Dingolfing, the former Glas factory, with the fresh-looking new models having a bodywork production line of their own, then transferring to share a line with the other models for the rest of the assembly. UK right-hand drive versions would be available a few months later, with road testing in the UK starting in the early summer of 1973.

Driving a solitary pilot-build 520 on BMW's brand-new Aschheim proving ground at launch time, *Autocar* magazine stated of the car's steering: "The steering felt as precise as all but the best rack and pinion systems, and remained light as long as the car was driven sedately. When it was pushed, the effort needed rose in a nicely progressive way to remind the driver what he was up to."The only snag mentioned was the slight jerkiness encountered from the throttle linkage as it proved difficult to obtain a smooth delivery of power. "Visibility from the driver's seat was first class," it continued, made so much better by slim A-post pillars, which we miss so much today. The 520's main European rivals were the home-built Audi 100, Opel Rekord and Commodore, Ford Granada and smaller Mercedes saloons. Built further afield, there was the French Peugeot 504 and Chrysler 180, then 2-litre, Swedish Volvo 144, Italian Alfa Romeo 2000 Berlina and, from the UK, it appealed to the same customers as the Rover P6 and Triumph 2000/2500 models.

New safety measures placed into the monocoque all-steel bodywork made the car heavier than the 2000, again almost approaching the weight of the 2500. Rolling down the early part of the production line in untrimmed form, an observer would have seen strong seat mounting employed but little evidence of cross-bracing inside the passenger compartment. Further strength came from the newly designed transmission tunnel and deep sills. The wings were bolted on, and the front and rear ends were designed to collapse progressively in an accident with predetermined 'crumple kinks' in the metal work to protect passengers in an emergency.

More subtle use of chrome was adopted, with all windows making good use of the brightwork. Throughflow ventilation was made possible by black plastic vents at the bases of the C-pillars, and the wider wheels used attractive chrome hubcaps with the BMW motif in the centre. Wheelarches still featured the flared 'eyebrow' look, as many cars did then.

The 520 was initially produced with a developed version of the four-cylinder 1990cc unit, but now with a choice of twin Stromberg CD carburettors or Kugelfischer fuel injection (the 520i) and higher compression ratio, tailored to meet the requirements of Germany's low-lead fuels. Numerous modifications were performed to the engine to produce almost as much power as the existing 2.5-litre unit, with the previous 2000 model only achieving an extra 5hp from its twin-choke Weber installation!

Non-overdrive five-speed gearboxes were largely still a future feature on most cars at this point, and the new 5 Series was fitted with a four-speed gearbox as standard from the outset or an optional five-speed manual or three-speed ZF automatic gearbox (costing just over £300 on top). The standard four-speed manual gearbox used slightly closer ratios than the previous 2000 model, but the final drive ratio was retained at 4.11. The all-round independent suspension was largely familiar, with MacPherson struts at the front with trailing arms at the rear mounted on an all-new second subframe. The concentric coil suspension allowed for a large 8in of suspension travel and was tilted and offset in relation to the centreline. With four-lamp tungsten halogen lights, a heated rear window and other possible drains, the electrical system was charged by an uprated alternator capable of keeping the battery topped up to the correct level at all times.

The six-cylinder 5 Series cars were introduced in 1973, with sales figures similar to the four-cylinder vehicles. Both models used the same sheet metalwork. Power came from the big 2.5- and 2.8-litre models, the 525 developing 145bhp from the 2494cc engine and the 528i 176bhp from the 2788cc unit. Four-wheel disc brakes were fitted to six-cylinder models and many were ordered with automatic transmission. The lucky US market got the 530i, the flagship of the 5 Series range with the federalised detoxed 2985cc engine, and the American magazine *Road & Track* stated it to be one of the world's top ten cars ever. It lasted until 1979. An economy 1.8-litre 518 joined the model range in 1974, taking advantage of company car taxation classes.

Facelifted models were identified in the autumn of 1976, with a revised bonnet being pressed that made the front grille appear to be taller and resembled the new E21 model. Alpina produced a super-rare 3.3-litre conversion of the standard 5 Series. In late 1979, BMW Motorsport announced perhaps what is considered to be the first BMW M car: the mighty 3.5-litre M535i. Produced between April 1980 and until the end of E12 production in July 1981, this had modified sports suspension, a power output of 218bhp allowing for a 0-60mph of 7.1 seconds and, if ordered as such, had red and blue pinstripes all round matching the revised front and rear seating that boasted the same style of stripes vertically. Just 1650 were produced, also identified by a revised bib spoiler up front and wider indicators. It is certainly collectable and a wolf in sheep's clothing!

E12 5 SERIES BODY TYPES: Four-door saloon. **Manufactured at:** Munich and CKD South Africa. **Number produced:** 738,000. **Production span:** 1972-1981.
PERFORMANCE (520I): Top speed: 116mph/km/h; **0-60mph/100km/h:** 10.5 seconds; **average economy:** 25mpg.
PRICE AT LAUNCH: £3559 (520i).
MEASUREMENTS: Length: 15ft ¼in (4.58m); **height:** 4ft 8in (1.42m); **width:** 5ft 6½in (1.69m); **wheelbase:** 8ft 7½in (2.63m); **kerb weight:** 2759lb (1254kg); **wheels:** 14in; **turning circle:** 33ft 0in (10.06m); **fuel capacity:** 12.5 gallons/56 litres; **boot capacity:** 17ft^3.
TECHNICAL: Engine types: 1766 and 1990cc four-cylinder and 1990, 2494, 2788 and 3453cc six-cylinder petrol; **gearbox:** four-speed manual; **suspension:** independent with MacPherson struts, lower wishbones, coil springs (front), independent semi-trailing arms, coil springs (rear); **brakes:** disc front and rear.
TRIM: Nylon velour.

E12 advertising slogans

Why people who own a BMW enjoy driving more than you do (528, 1977)
Fast car – faster chassis
Cool, calm and collected
How many people actually enjoy going to work?
BMW. The car company that hasn't been legislated into mediocrity (whole range)
The luxury sedan that did not have to be re-engineered to face difficult times (USA)
A car that meets the demands of the 80s without violating the concept of a BMW
A luxury sedan based on the belief that all of the rich are not idle
Meeting the demands of society is no excuse for building a boring car
The BMW is built for roads you'd be wise to avoid in your present luxury sedan
Why people who own a BMW enjoy driving more than you do
The BMW 530i. Based on the belief that a true luxury car is more than a living room with white walls
The BMW 530i. An engineer's conception of a luxury car, not an interior decorator's
No other company gives you so much change for your money (1981 model range)
We took the heart out of our racing car… and put it in a new body. The new BMW M535i.

E28 5 Series

After an impressive near three quarters of a million production run of the E12 5 Series, the new E28 models were launched in the summer of 1981, and many models such as the 518 and 528 SE did not see their way onto UK shores until the next year. The E28 cars sat lower than the E12s within a slightly shorter wheelbase, despite visually looking very similar to their predecessors, and appeared to be more of a facelift than a replacement. Indeed the only panels that were the same were the door skins and roof panel, with new dashboards (answering the criticisms of the old one that had untidy air vents everywhere) and refreshed interiors for the 11 per cent price hike. The bonnet was all new, now more steeply raked to aid in aerodynamics. Overall they were 200lb lighter than the previous E12 and, despite similar dimensions, afforded extra interior room for the occupants.

Initially, power was available in either four cylinders (the rather basic equipment 518 had a single 1766cc engine in either single Pierburg carburettor or Bosch L-Jetronic fuel-injected form as the 518i), or six-cylinder format (1990, 2490, 2788 and 3420cc engines). The top model was initially the 130mph 528i, which heavily rivalled the Audi 200T, with the high specification 528i SE being equipped with anti-lock braking, electric steel sliding sunroof, headlamp wash wipe and high-specification computer. *Motor* magazine tested an early production example in November 1981 and concluded: "It is an even more satisfying car than its predecessor,

The dashboard arrangement for the 5 Series.

The M5 E28 displaying alloy wheels, headlamp washers and front fog lights.

and neither are its passengers neglected, for with the exceptions of its mediocre ride, the engine noise when revved, the 528i is a comfortable and civilised machine in which to travel."Gearboxes were five-speed only in Getrag manual format, with initially a three-speed automatic gearbox until the introduction of the 535i when automatics were uprated to four-speed format.

Hot on the heels of the 528i's launch was a specially tuned 145mph TWR 3.5-litre version from Tom Walkinshaw Racing in the UK. The engine was blueprinted, the cylinder head reworked and the bodywork benefited from front and rear spoilers that were body-coloured, as were the mirrors. A new one would set you back £18,500 in 1982.

The age of the car computer was here. The E28 had an ingenious system of knowing when the model needed servicing, as it monitored the number of cold starts and how often high revs were applied to the engine. A trip computer was also fitted, not unlike that used in the 7 Series, this even predicting an arrival time for the destination, although a far cry from today's live traffic maps and timing and route calculations based on the movements of thousands of smartphones.

In the 1983 and 1984 model years, the Japanese and American markets also got the 533i, a high-specification six-cylinder car that was replaced by the 535i. Diesels and sport models came later. Perhaps the oddball cars in the range were the 525e and 528e produced between 1983 and 1987, largely with the American and Japanese market in mind but, after a year, also sold in the UK and Europe.

In this case the 'e' stood for *eta*, a Greek word for efficiency. Almost like a design forerunner to the electric i3 in 2012, these models also used skinny tyres (175HR/14) to aid in helping with a lower drag coefficient. They had the low-friction 2.7-litre engine that gave 115mph but could also attain 35mpg – but not at the same time ... Transmission was a rather high-geared four-speed automatic gearbox with automatic lock-up for top gear. The 525e and 528e cars did not really stand well in most people's perception of what BMW was all about, but sold for four years, sporting plastic wheel trims over steel wheels in some markets.

The rear aspect of the later 5 Series with larger rear lamp clusters.

The model range was later expanded by sport models between 1985 and 1987. After a four-year gap, the M535i was back, and sold just over 2200 models, making it rather exclusive. A very creditable 152mph was achievable, and a stunning acceleration figure of 0-60mph in around 6.4 seconds. Flared wheelarches, M Technic spoilers, side skirts and, soon after launch, M Technic suspension was fitted. The 3430cc car today is an appreciating asset, making the UK weekly magazine *Motor*'s front cover at launch time. The model had a Bosch ME Motronic engine management system. A non-M derivative, the 535i, was also offered, with the American version known as the 535iS. Alpina was also back on the 5 Series scene with its rorty B10, described by many as a near-perfect Q saloon.

The new (with 3453cc engine from the racing M1) M5 was produced at the same time as the M535i. Initially, a 210kW M88/3 version existed, and the S38

A nice example of a 520i seen at a Suffolk classic car event. The rear lamps (above) on the E46 were larger than those on the E28. The twin round lamps on the European models could also be used for the American market without making any adjustments for legal reasons.

version with 191kW for the federal US market soon followed. These were both produced until 1988, and 150 were destined for the UK at around £32,000. It was identified by discreet badging on the radiator grille and wider-profile 220/55VR 390 tyres, but by little else save for the big M-Power name cast on the cylinder head. Internally there was a full-leather buffalo hide interior extending to the seats, door panels, centre console and lower dash panel and, underneath, a 25 per cent limited-slip differential to help stop wheelspin.

Left: A 525e speeds past the camera, this one in 1987.
Below: The same car, from the rear driver's side, and displaying the 525e badging.

Acceleration was a stunning 0-60mph time of just 6 seconds, but overall fuel consumption suffered, with test cars averaging around 16mpg. It was, at the time, the ultimate practical and sensible homologation special. *Autocar* magazine performance tested one on the German autobahn, achieving a stunning average two-way speed of 153mph, or just 14.3 seconds per kilometre!

A diesel version was added to the 5 Series E28 range in 1983. This turbo 524td version used the 2433cc engine with indirect injection and a Garrett turbocharger to produce 115bhp and was launched at the Geneva Motor Show that year. A derv-powered BMW was a novelty at the time. Reaching 112mph (180km/h) was certainly achievable, with a somewhat lazy-sounding 0-60mph of around 13 seconds. An even slower 85bhp non-turbo diesel, the 524d, joined the model range for about a year until the demise of the E28 5 Series in 1987, but this was something of a rarity, only available in certain European markets. Overall, 722,328 5 Series E28 models were produced in a six-year production run, all in four-door saloon form. The model gave way to the new longer-wheelbase E34 5 Series from 1988, covered later in this book.

E28 5 SERIES BODY TYPES: Four-door saloon. **Manufactured at:** Munich. **Number produced:** 722,328. **Production span:** 1981-1987.
PERFORMANCE (M535I): Top speed: 143mph/210km/h; 0-60mph/100km/h: 7.4 seconds; **average economy:** 18mpg.
PRICE AT LAUNCH: £11,745 (528i).
MEASUREMENTS: Length: 15ft 2in (4.66m); **height:** 4ft 8in (1.42m); **width:** 5ft 5in (1.65m); **wheelbase:** 8ft 8in (2.64m); **kerb weight:** 3326lb (1509kg); **wheels:** 14in; **turning circle:** 33ft 6in (10.22m); **fuel capacity:** 15.4 gallons/70 litres; **boot capacity:** 17ft^3.
TECHNICAL: Engine types: 1766 and 1990cc four-cylinder and 2693, 2494, 2788, 3430 and 3453cc six-cylinder petrol, 2443cc diesel; **gearbox:** four-speed manual; **suspension:** independent with MacPherson strut, coil

springs, anti-roll bar (front), independent by semi-trailing arms, coil springs, anti-roll bars (rear); **brakes:** disc front and rear.

TRIM: Velour.
KEY OPTIONAL EXTRAS: Automatic transmission, headlamp wash wipe.

E28 media slogans

It thinks, it remembers, it communicates. No wonder it was on News At Ten every night for a week (1981)
Introducing the forerunner of imitations to come
The first known example of a car evaluating its driver
Test drive a BMW 5 Series. Now be honest. How does you own car feel? (picture of a sponge)
What's the right price for a BMW 5 Series? (Lots of guesses in the script...)
Don't touch the brakes. Don't touch the cones. And don't touch this test in any other £10,000 car.
How to bring a BMW 520i more in line with its rivals
How much would you like this BMW 5 Series to be when finished?
Shouldn't you have brakes that can tell the difference?
Introducing the car conventional wisdom decreed could not be built
BMW believe you should know your brake lights don't work before he does (Artic close behind in mirror)
A car that reflects achievement not merely social acceptance
BMW transforms the automobile into a higher form of intelligence
Three of the most sophisticated power plants in the world aren't nuclear
Introducing the car that blurs the distinction between racing machines and luxury sedans
The new 535 is. It isn't the first car to use an air dam and a spoiler. Just the most qualified.

The Alpina B3 was based on the E46 5 Series.

1975-1993 – 3 SERIES (E21 & E30)

E21, 1975-1982 3 Series

The Munich Olympic Stadium was again used as the venue for the launch of the new 3 Series in June 1975. The 3 Series was the second range of cars to gain the new style of badging, after the E12 5 Series had pioneered this in 1972. The styling of the 3 Series was overseen by Paul Bracq, the director of design at BMW. Out now was the 1960s look of angular corners, high waist-lines and copious use of chrome detailing of the 02 series.

The E21 was intended to represent the entry-level series into BMW, although as described elsewhere in these pages the 02 lived on as the economy 1502 and was produced alongside the 3 Series for a couple more years. Colours of the new models were often very bright, this being the trend of the day by all the major manufacturers in Europe. The E21 was just produced in three-door format on a 102in wheelbase and no estate version was sold on the E21 platform. Carburettor models only were seen at launch, with Bosch K-Jetronic fuel-injection cars being added to the range within a few months. All models (at least until the 323i later on) came with front disc brakes and rear drums, and had all-independent suspension.

The BMW 316, the entry-level E21 model, was not available on all markets.

The 3 Series initially comprised the following models in 1975:

316 – with 1.6-litre 89bhp M10 engine: £2799
318 – with 1.8-litre 97bhp M10 engine: Not in UK
320 – with 2-litre M10 engine, dual headlamps: £3349
Note – automatic option: +£275

Press reviews were enthusiastic, with

A new E21 under test. All this series were offered as two-door saloons only.

particularly favourable comments on the new-style dashboard that became a trademark feature of BMW interiors for a long time. This and the centre console were now angled toward the driver, the idea copied by many other manufacturers, such as Opel, which adopted it for its series 2 Monza and Senator cars from 1983. By introducing fuel-injection initially to the 320 then from 1980 the 318, with the 320i models running alongside the carburettor 320 model, performance generally improved. Acceleration was normally around a second quicker to 60mph and top speed was normally improved by around 5mph, but his came at a cost, with such models costing approximately 10 per cent more. A wise option was that of a limited-slip differential to the fuel-injected cars.

Thus the new models were to become 318i and 320i, with the entry-level 316 staying in normally aspirated

Above: 1978 US advertising, and left: 1981 US advertising with the bigger bumpers.

form and UK versions keeping the carburettor form only. The carburettor 318 was dropped in favour of the fuel-injected 318i cars. There were some confusing models, however: in the US, the 320 model no longer used the M20 four-cylinder engine, and the 320/6 was marketed, now fitted with a six-cylinder engine fed by a four-barrel downdraught carburettor by Solex. This was the first E21 in the US with a six-pot arrangement; in Sweden the 1.8-litre 318i was badged as 320i, and identified by twin headlamps, due to the 2-litre engine not passing the tough Swedish emission tests.

Introduced with a 2.3-litre six-cylinder fuel-injected M60 engine, the new 323i could whisk the model from 0 to 60mph in just over 8½ seconds, and achieved an easy 118mph top

Top left: UK-specification 1981 316; top right: the front aspect of the same car. Bottom left: 165/80 R13 tyres fitted to the 316, and bottom right: the rear aspect of this remarkably unaltered example.

speed. The rear drum brakes from the rest of the range were replaced by discs for added safety and new options included power steering and a dogleg sport Getrag five-speed manual gearbox. The M3 badge was never seen on an E21 body. The 323i was the flagship of the range from 1977 until 1982, and cost around 38 per cent more in the UK than the 316 base model when it became available here in the UK from 1979 in manual-only form:

316	£5004
320	£6335
323i	£7399

Again in 1977, the 320 was marketed in the US with fuel-injection and, by 1980, was downsized to 1.8 litres. Visually to many Europeans' eyes, the necessary federal changes made to the compact 3 Series never really sat well, with revised bumpers that increased its length by 6in, bigger indicators, side reflectors and sealed beam headlamps.

Between 1978 and 1981, a stylish convertible version of the 3 Series was available from Baur, which had previously offered conversions on the 02 series. The Top Cabriolet had an ingenious Targa roof

Baur convertible with the roof up.

arrangement that could be stowed in the boot, and came with separate folding rear soft top similar to the Triumph Stag. Over 4500 examples were built with full BMW warranty backing, and any engine configuration could be specified, usually at a cost of around £2600 extra.

2500 320 iS models were produced in white, silver or black from 1981, a 3 Series with optional 'S' package. Air-conditioning was deleted on this model and a resultant storage area appeared in the central dashboard to take its place. Standard equipment included:

Leather-wrapped steering wheel (three-spoke)
Cross-spoke alloy wheels
Front air dam with integrated fog lamps
Rear badge deletion
Getrag five-speed transmission
Limited-slip differential
Anti-roll bars all-round, stiffened at the front
Recaro front seats
Leather gearshift knob
Manually operated sunroof
Uprated Blaupunkt radio/cassette player

The 315, a rarely seen 74bhp economy 3 Series, was added to the range for certain markets from early 1981 and continued in the price lists alongside the new E30 until 1984. Perhaps aimed at fleet buyers and car hire outlets, it retained the same 1.6-litre engine as the 316 but price savings were obvious – with certain trim deletions such as map pockets in the doors, no carpet on the rear shelf, cheaper R2 headlamps and a single external door mirror. The bumpers were cheaper too, displaying exposed screws.

Production ceased of the first generation of BMW 3 Series by the end of 1983, moving to concentrate on the new E30 models, after 1.3 million cars had been produced.

E21 3 SERIES BODY TYPES: Two-door saloon. **Manufactured at:** Munich. **Number produced:** 1,364,000 (approximate including CKD kits). **Production span:** 1974-1981.
PERFORMANCE (316 BASE MODEL): **Top speed:** 100mph/160km/h; **0-60mph/100km/h:** 12.8 seconds; **average economy:** 25-35mpg.
PRICE AT LAUNCH: £2799/£3979 (316 and 320i in 1976).
MEASUREMENTS: **Length:** 14ft 3in (4.34m); **height:** 4ft 6in (1.37m); **width:** 5ft 3in (1.6m); **wheelbase:** 8ft 4in (2.54m); **kerb weight:** 2193lb (995kg); **wheels:** 13in; **turning circle:** 29ft 6in (9m); **fuel capacity:** 11.4 gallons/52 litres; **boot capacity:** 10.3ft^3.
TECHNICAL: **Engine types:** 1573, 1563, 1766 and 1977cc four-cylinder 1990 and

1979 US advertising for the 320i S with the larger spoiler.

2315cc six-cylinder petrol; **gearbox:** four-speed manual; **suspension:** independent with MacPherson struts, coil springs and anti-roll bar (front), independent with MacPherson struts, coil springs and semi-trailing arms (rear); **brakes:** disc front, drum rear.
TRIM: Velour.

Another pristine UK 3 Series.

E21 advertising slogans
If it rained less on a £6,000 BMW than a £22,000 BMW, we'd give it less paint (316 and 735i)
Country Life
A quarter of the time we spend building a BMW we spend painting it (316i)
The BMW cabriolet. The sun on your face without the wind in your hair
Logik der Abgrenzung/Logic of demarcation
Le droit au plaisir/The right to pleasure
Auf-Rechnung/On bill
Die Kunst, mit Erfolgndivualist zu sein/The art of being an individualist with success
Siate esigenti/Be demanding (320)
In a BMW, the driver is not asked to compensate for the shortcomings of the automobile (320i)
Shaken. Not stirred (320i)
Introducing the successor that started a cult (320i)
BMW. One of the few car companies not currently introducing imitation BMWs (320i)
Now you don't have to trade in your family to own a sports car (320i S)
Le nuove BMW 320, 323i: progreesso sostanziale/The new BMW 320, 323i: substantial progress
The sedan that defined performance for a generation of cars unfamiliar with the term
Also available in 118 less racy colours (323i)
For the joy of motoring (323i)
Leave yesterday behind (320, 1980s)
Is it a 3 Series on the road, or another £6,000 car on the production line? (1981)

E30, 1982-1994 3 Series

It was way back in 1978 that the final design of the new E30 3 Series BMW was signed off. Designers Claus Luthe and Boyke Boyer used CAD (computer-aided design) to perfect the revised model, which very much resembled the successful E21, but this time the design team was to introduce a much-needed estate car, and, like the 02 range, the Touring name was adopted for such models. Also, to improve market share, saloons came in both two- and four-door format, and an attractive convertible was available. For sporting motoring, Alpine conversions were offered again, but these were somewhat overshadowed by the new high-profile M3

Thankfully, most classic cars seem to adopt the standard 'as-built' look, like this 1983/4 316 E30.

The next E30 generation of 3 Series was also available with four doors. This is another fine example of a two-door, however, with deeper box spoiler. Photographed in 2024.

which made its debut in 1986. The best sales year was 1986, when nearly a third of a million E30s were produced.

Gearboxes varied depending on the specific specification of the model. There were four-speed Getrag manual boxes on the 316 and 318s, and three five-speed manual boxes fitted to the rest of the range. ZF automatics came in as both three and four-speed, the former being deleted in 1985.

Autocar magazine tested an early 320i in a February 1983 issue and commented, "The engine is a jewel. It is fast, exceptionally efficient, and generally quiet. It is among the best built cars in this class and now has better (if not perfect) handling. It is likely to appeal to those who enjoy the handling qualities inherent in rear-wheel drive."

Across the various markets, the complete engine range at the launch was:

1.6-litre (four-cylinder) for the 316 / 316i	1982-1987	M10B16
1.8-litre (four-cylinder) for the 316/318	1982-1988	M10B18
2.0-litre (six-cylinder) for the 320i	1982-1985	M20B20
2.3-litre (six-cylinder) for the 323i	1982-1984	M20
Following on with:		
2.7-litre (six-cylinder) for the 325	1985-1988	M20B27
2.5-litre (six-cylinder) for the 325	1985-1993	M20B25
2.3-litre (four-cylinder) for the M3 and Evo 1/2	1986-1988	S14B23
2.5-litre (four-cylinder) for the M3 Sport Evo	1989-1990	S14B25
2.4-litre (six-cylinder diesel) for the 324d	1985-1993	M21

Standard BMW alloy wheels on this E30.

A late-model 318 is factory-convertible.

A six-cylinder 325i rear badge.

A 325i convertible with the roof open, showing off its wooden facia.

All fuel-injected engines were by now L-Jetronic systems.

The 324d diesel

As diesel-powered cars became more tax-efficient for company car drivers, more made their way onto the marketplace. BMW's M21 engine had been fitted to the 5 Series since 1983, and in 1985 was fitted into the 3 Series to become the 324d. This model was more economical and appealed to the long-distance sales rep.

M3 and Evolution

To represent the sporting end of the E30 series, the 1986-1990 M3 used the 2302cc in-line six engine with Bosch Motronic engine management and produced 200bhp. It attained 146mph and a 0-60mph acceleration figure of 7.6 seconds. The chassis had been comprehensively revised by the BMW internal team led by Thomas Ammersschlager. He had been headhunted from Audi having worked on the Quattro, and previously with Zakspeed racing, famed for its turbocharged racing Capris. Many suspension changes were made, particularly regarding the placement of the components and beefier coil springs. A dogleg pattern Getrag gearbox was fitted in European

Only 480 examples of the Johnny Cecetto limited-edition M3 were built.

A UK press picture of an early E30 M3, easily identified by its blister arches and revised front and rear spoilers.

models, while US cars used the box from the 325i Sport, fearing the Americans would not favour an unusually patterned stick-shift. A lighter shell, front and rear spoilers and flared Quattro-style wheelarches were used to complete the sporting, aggressive look. Further changes were made to the line of the boot lid resulting in a shallower rear window line, all to aid in high-speed aerodynamics.

Using the stronger hubs from its bigger stablemates, the M3s had five stud wheels. Amazingly, a convertible version of the M3 was also built. In New Zealand, the M3 was never sold, however, a local importer there created about 100 of its own sporty versions named the M325i.

Worldwide track racing with the M3 started in 1987, and it won many races. In late

The cockpit of the E30 M3 in left-hand drive form.

The M3 cabriolet made a fine long-distance fresh-air tourer. This one dates to 1987.

1988, a new M3 Evolution model satisfied the homologation regulations, where 5000 were needed, and 40 of these came to the UK, again all in left-hand drive form. This £26,960 miniature supercar represented less value for money than the standard M3 at £23,550, with a top speed of 146mph and 0-60mph in just 6.6 seconds.

The four-wheel drives and other specials

The iX badge on the rear of a BMW denotes all-wheel drive, not to be confused with later BMW X cars that use four-wheel drive. In the E30 range, the six-cylinder 2.5-litre 325 iX had very little marketing, but proved very popular and was the first production BMW badged as such. It was also made available in the US. The Alpina C1, C2, B3 and B6 models were built at Buchloe between 1987 and 1992 with the B3 based on the 325i platform with the M20 engine and also available as a cabriolet in limited numbers. It also produced its version of the M3, with a significantly revised 3430cc engine. In all, 257 units were built.

An interesting E30 from 1985 to 1987 was the 333i from South Africa's Motorsport division. This had the 197hp 3.2-litre M30 big-six engine in a two-door model and was successful in local saloon car racing. Due to a lack of room, drivers had a choice – either order it with power steering or air-conditioning, but not both! It achieved around 142mph on the track and 204 cars were produced. Another notable E30 was the black and gold 323i JPS (John Player Special Edition) from Australia, a limited edition built as a tribute to race cars competing in local touring car racing.

E30 3 SERIES BODY TYPES: Two-door and four-door saloon, five-door estate, Baur conversion and factory cabriolet. **Manufactured at:** Munich, and four-cylinder 316 cars in CKD form in Rosslyn, South Africa until 1992. **Number produced:** 2,433,000 approx. **Production span:** 1982-1992, but convertibles to 1993 and estate to 1994. (1982-1991 in the US).
PERFORMANCE (320I): Top speed: 119mph/190km/h; **0-60mph/100km/h:** 8 seconds; **average economy:** 28mpg.
PRICE AT LAUNCH: £9588 (320i).
MEASUREMENTS: Length: 14ft 2¼in (4.32m); **height:** 4ft 4½in (1.38m); **width:** 5ft 5in (1.64m); **wheelbase:** 8ft 5½in (2.57m); **kerb weight:** 2432lb (1103kg); **wheels:** 14in; **turning circle:** 29ft 6in (9m); **fuel capacity:** 12 gallons/55 litres; **boot capacity:** 15ft^3.
TECHNICAL: Engine types: 1596, 1766,

1990cc four-cylinder 2302, 2316, 2494, 2693cc six-cylinder petrol, 2443cc six-cylinder diesel; **gearbox:** four- and five-speed manual; four and five-speed automatic; **suspension:** independent with MacPherson struts, coil springs and anti-roll bar (front), independent with MacPherson struts, coil springs, anti-roll bar and semi-trailing arms (rear); **brakes:** disc front, drum rear (M3 disc at rear)

TRIM: Velour.

KEY OPTIONAL EXTRAS: Limited-slip differential, manual sunroof, electric windows, green tinted glass, central locking, sunroof, damper control, headlamp wash/wipe.

E30 advertising slogans

It might pass for a BMW. Until it passes you (Alpina C2 cabrio 323, 1988)
How would you like a BMW 3 Series?
Is it a BMW on the road, or another £6000 car on the production line?
For once, BMW have nothing to add (316i Lux)
BMW introduce a sports saloon for children (four-door)
Now there's more than one way into a BMW sports car (four-door)
The new BMW 318i gets him around 20% quicker
Proof that a £10,000 car costs less than a £9000 car (318i)
Only when you're behind the wheel does the new 318 iS show its true colours
The heavenly difference (cabriolet)
The next best thing to a new BMW (cabriolet)
It also holds its value (323i)
Curiously, it can now cost more to drive an imitation BMW than a BMW (325i)
For those of you who couldn't possibly drive an estate, BMW offer you three alternatives
Unashamedly individual (Hartge)
It's why some enthusiasts are more enthusiastic than others (325 iS)
M3 Media
Remember when £40,000 would buy a roof over your head? (M3 Cabriolet)
The gulf between BMW and its many would-be competitors can now be measured in cylinders (325es)
Superiority is not a secret (M3)
The M power play (M3)
24 hours, 3650 kilometres, triple victories (M3)
Our sport is perfection (M3)
Anything any sports sedan can do, this one does outrageously (M3)

1976-1999 – 6, 7 & 8 SERIES (E24, E23, E32, E31)

6 Series E24

Any visitor to the Geneva Motor Show in early 1976 would have been treated to a first glimpse of the new BMW 6 Series, now on show after an exhaustive three-year design period under Bernhard Osswald. The Swiss show was the platform used to launch the big new E24 series, also shown throughout the year at other venues. The new, sleek coupé model directly replaced the earlier E9 CS coupé series that had spawned the mighty 'Batmobile'; a tough nut to crack when it came to marketing an all-new car to the same customer base. The elegant E24 took on a more rounded and lower appearance, at a time when German competition was realising the potential of big six-cylinder coupés. Mercedes was already enjoying sales success with its big CE and SLC cars, and the soon-to-be-launched Opel Monza was just a couple of years away. Overall, the 6 Series E24 was longer, lower and wider than its predecessor, and afforded high handling and roadholding levels.

Initially the European range consisted of the 630 CS, a carburettor 3-litre, and the 633 CSi, a 3.3-litre with fuel injection. The US magazine *Road & Track* stated in 1977, "the engine, is without a doubt, the most sophisticated production in-line six in the world." Then, 30 months later the five-speed manual 140mph 635 CSi competed directly against the faster Mercedes 450 SLC 5.0. This became the top model, and was fitted with a black moulded rubber spoiler mounted on the boot and a stylish squarer front chin spoiler. Up front was a detuned M90 version of the 3.5-litre engine fitted to the earlier E9 model, and BMW advised buyers it was the fastest four-seat coupé made in Europe. Any references to the contemporary Porsche 928 were dismissed, as this was a 2+2 coupé. The American market proved difficult to conquer amid an unfortunate monetary exchange rate at the time, with only the fuel-injected 3-litre 630i available initially for a year, followed by the 633 CSi. Both models had a distinctly unsavoury-looking federal bumper setup that never seemed to suit the lines of any European manufactured car. The 3.5-litre version was never sold in the US.

The normally aspirated 630 CS was deleted from the 6 Series range in summer

A splendid 630 CS photographed when brand new. This was really a 2+2, as room in the back was limited, even for such a large car.

A cutaway line drawing of the new 6 Series as produced by the Munich factory upon launch.

1979, being replaced with another model in the line-up that made use of a high compression version of the 2.8-litre 528i engine. Thus the complete 6 Series range was now fuel-injected, all with L-Jetronic at first, followed by the better Motronic system. A Getrag five-speed manual gearbox was used from 1981 (with direct-drive fifth speed), replacing the earlier four-speed unit. If automatic transmission was ordered, the previous three-speed gearbox was uprated to four-speed in 1984.

In the summer of 1982, the 6 Series was fitted with new 23cc smaller 3430cc six-cylinder engine, with the new model named 635 CSi still capable of 142mph. It featured Motronic digital engine management and a closed throttle fuel cut-off to aid economy. ABS braking became standard fitting, and adopted from the 7 Series was the new driver's service indicator that electronically worked out how hard the engine had been driven, and when it was due for a service. Another feature inherited from the 7 Series was the revised offset Dopplegelenk suspension modifications. On directly comparing the 635 CSi with the competition, namely the Audi Quattro, Jaguar XJ-S HE, Mercedes 380 SEC, Opel Monza and Porche 928, *Autocar* road testers reported, "This leaves us with the mechanically smooth, powerful and efficient BMW. The engine's combination of performance and economy counts for a lot, so does the equipment fitted as standard – and finish."

The front aspect of a UK 6 Series.

It was not until September 1983 that the M635 CSi made its debut at the Frankfurt Motor Show with the somewhat rorty and further developed M88 3453cc engine with dual overhead camshafts that had featured in the M1 cars. It had a bigger bore and shorter stroke compared with its stablemates. Astonishingly, it would redline at 8000rpm, giving 286bhp at 6500rpm, allowing for 0-60mph acceleration times of around 6 seconds and a creditable 150mph. A low 583 M635 CSi models were sold in total, with Americans often referring to it as the M6. All 635s were available with a catalytic converter from autumn 1985, often ordered as such to allow for new German taxation advantages. In May 1987, the last major changes were made to the 6 Series after the deletion of the 628 entry model. Front spoilers now had

A 6 Series at the beach.

The interior of the 6 Series.

6 Series alloy wheel.

Note the fine leather upholstery.

The rear aspect of a 1983 635CSi Turbo track car.

integrated driving lamps fitted, and twin-tube gas dampers were added. Production ended in 1989, leaving a temporary coupé void for the BMW line-up before the new E31 8 Series arrived in 1990. In all, 86,216 had been produced in 13 years.

E24 6 SERIES BODY TYPES: Two-door coupé. **Manufactured at:** Munich. **Number produced:** 86,216 (M series equated to 5855). **Production span:** 1976-1989.

PERFORMANCE (635 CSI AUTOMATIC): **Top speed:** 135mph/220km/h; **0-60mph/100km/h:** 7.5 seconds; **average economy:** 19-24mpg.
PRICE AT LAUNCH: £14,599 (633 CSi).
MEASUREMENTS: **Length:** 15ft 7¼in (4.75m); **height:** 4ft 5½in (1.36m); **width:** 5ft 8in (1.72m); **wheelbase:** 8ft 7½in (2.63m); **kerb weight:** 3197lb (1450kg); **wheels:** 15in; **turning circle:** 34ft 3in (10.4m); **fuel capacity:**

The interior of the 6 Series shown here was often a challenge for adults to endure on a long journey, proving unfavourable compared to a rival car, the German Opel Monza, which was built at the same time.

The badging and boot spoiler of the 635CSi.

Twin headlamps with factory wash wipes fitted.

The interior of a 635CSi track car.

Above: The distinctive upright kidney grille (6 Series).

An immaculate 1980s UK 6 Series photographed in 2024.

The M635CSi version.

The frontal aspect of the 6 Series seems absolutely timeless in this 2024 picture.

A European model M635CSi.

15.4 gallons/70 litres; **boot capacity:** 18.7ft^3.
TECHNICAL: Engine types: 2788, 2986, 3210 and 3453cc six-cylinder petrol; **gearbox:** five-speed manual or four-speed automatic; **suspension:** MacPherson strut with coil (front), semi-trailing arms (rear); **brakes:** discs front and rear.
TRIM: Velour, leather.

A UK press advert for the 3.5-litre limited-edition M635CSi. "Anyone can dream. Only 40 can buy."

The rear aspect of the M635CSi at a classic car show in Felixstowe.

The front aspect of the super-rare Alpina model 6 Series.

The M635CSi sits between earlier M1 and later M6 cars.

E24 advertising slogans

The true test of a fast car is how well it performs slowly (6 Series. 1980s)
Addiction (633, 1977)
It also has brains (635 CSi, 1988)
A £35,000 BMW. An £8,000 BMW (or is it the other way round?) (316 and M635CSi, 1980s
The new 1982 BMW coupe. Even rarer than a 1929 Chateau Lafite
The true grand touring tradition has come within one car of extinction
It takes a company as advanced as BMW to make 2+2 = 4
As close to an all-out racing machine as a passenger car should ever come
A luxury coupé that offers more than the mere illusion of high performance
The new BMW 633 coupé reflects the qualities that make people successful
How to tell a true grand touring coupé from cars hoping to be mistaken for one
Variations on the same theme
Nothing succeeds like success
BMW's racing engine is now available to a wider public. But not much wider (with track cars)
Acknowledged Masters
If life is a journey, then life's greatest tragedy is not having enjoyed the trip
Perhaps the only luxury coupé whose performance lives up to its price

7 Series E23

From January 1977, the big six-cylinder 6 Series models were joined by a new long-wheelbase-only four-door stablemate, the 7 Series E23, of similar design and appearance, which had been conceived as long back as 1970, with a long design period following. A prime objective of Bernhard Osswold for this model was to improve comfort, silence and safety over the previous six-cylinder saloons. Early prototypes were being tested in 1971 at the new test facility at Aschheim, with particular emphasis being placed on the new suspension setup, and authorisation for a cobbled batch of pre-production prototypes came in September 1972, just as the earlier model 3.0 CSL and contemporary 5 Series entered production. The new body design was signed off in May 1974 and, in late 1975, full prototypes were being built and commonly referred to in the factory as the 7 Series. After thorough testing, by 1976 designs were finalised for all the machine tooling, and efforts were made by the marketing department to finalise trim levels and the model range for a May 1977 launch.

A rarely seen UK press advert for the 7 Series. This one features as an approved used car.

An American 1979 733i press advertisement: "Performance and efficiency can coexist under the same hood."

Three initial models were available: the 728, 730 and 733i. There was also a 725 on the continent. Public reception was good, with 3300 being built a month, and the manual versions proving faster than the Mercedes 450 SEL and 12-cylinder Jaguar XJs that were automatic only. However, a three-speed automatic was available which changed the whole character of the new model, albeit resulting in it being slower than its competition. *Road & Track* stated, "the engine doesn't feel that well matched to the automatic." *Motor* concluded in its 1977 test, "Overall, then, the 728 is an impressive machine, as well it should be at the price."

The rear aspect of a European 733i.

Fuel economy and performance improvements were seen in 1979 with compression ratios of all models being increased to 9.3:1. The 3.0 carburettor engine was discontinued from the range, while the single Solex 2.8-litre car gained electronic fuel injection and was renamed 728i. The unusually badged 733i was renamed to a more correct 732i designation. An executive express 735i model with the 3430cc engine was also added to the 7 Series family using a 218bhp M90 engine allowing for a creditable 135mph. Five-speed manual Getrag transmission was now offered on US cars, already seen on European models for a while, and a capacious shooting brake estate version was added to the American line-up for 1982.

Just as the 6 Series gained improvements in September 1983, the 7 Series was not forgotten. Healthy 15-20 per cent fuel gains were made across the range as the drag coefficient figure was reduced by 13 per cent (a mildly revised style front end was used) and the cars were around 250lb (110kg) lighter overall. A major factor in the improved economy was a lockable torque converter now fitted to the four-speed automatic ZF gearbox, similar to that of the German Opel Monza and Senators which also gained better economy at around the same time. A significant suspension update was announced

The onboard computer of the 745i.

A later-model European-spec 733i.

too for 1983: the front end received double-pivot geometry and changes were made to the angles of the rear trailing arms to accommodate a Trac-Link arrangement. The 138mph hot rod of the 7 Series, the 745i turbocharged saloon with 3210cc engine, also joined the range in limited-production form in 1980.

It was hoped, in the early 1970s, to have produced a V8 or V12-powered top model, but the extra weight and dreadful fuel economy (16mpg on test vehicles) negated this (at least at this point!), especially in view of the 1973-74 fuel crises. The 745i gained useful extra performance for the non-speed-limited autobahns and extra uprated disc brakes for descending those Alpine mountains. Ten a day were built (although in reality the market was not that strong even for that number), and incredibly the engine was made larger in September 1983 to 3430cc with new Motronic II engine management. The original 7 Series BMW continued until 1986, when over 285,000 units had been built, three times the volume of the 6 Series.

E23 7 SERIES BODY TYPES: Four-door saloon. **Manufactured at:** Munich and Rosslyn. **Number produced:** 285,368. **Production span:** 1977-1986.
PERFORMANCE (728): Top speed: 121mph/195km/h; **0-60mph/100km/h:** 9 seconds; **average economy:** 20mpg.
PRICE AT LAUNCH: £8950 (728).
MEASUREMENTS: Length: 15ft 11¼in (4.86m); **height:** 4ft 6½in (1.43m); **width:** 5ft 11in (1.8m); **wheelbase:** 9ft 2in (2.79m); **kerb weight:** 3241lb (1470kg); **wheels:** 14in; **turning circle:** 35ft 6in (9m); **fuel capacity:** 18.7 gallons/84.5 litres; **boot capacity:** 12.6ft^3.
TECHNICAL: Engine types: 2.5, 2.8, 3.0, 3.2, 3.4-litre six-cylinder petrol; **gearbox:** four and five-speed manual, three and four-speed automatic; **suspension:** independent by MacPherson struts, anti-roll bar and coils (front), independent by semi-trailing arms and coils (rear); **brakes:** disc front and rear.
TRIM: Velour, leather.
KEY OPTIONAL EXTRAS: Central locking, alloy road wheels.

E23 advertising slogans

It's tuned 100 times every second. Instead of once every 10,000 miles (1981)
1976, 1977, 1978, 1979, 1980, 1981: Lap of honour. 1981: Lap of luxury (1981)
Reality is the moment when one buys a BMW rather than a car (1979)
Like their drivers, capability exceeds demand (730)
For those who've come a long way and intend to go considerably further
A question of style
Status or purpose
The programme of contrasts
The ideals behind success
Before you buy a BMW 7 Series, you should listen to its critics (735i)

7 Series E32

A second series of 7 Series cars, the E32, was launched in May 1986 with the advent of the new 735i, and the 730i six months later. In-house styling was overseen by Claus Luthe, starting as way back as 1979. From the rear it was easily identified by its L-shaped tail lights. The model range was now initially limited to just two engine sizes, again both in-line six-cylinder, the 118bhp 2986cc and 211bhp 3430cc petrol units with fuel injection, finally leaving any carburettor models in the past.

Soon also available were 5-litre V12 M70 and V8 M60 engines. There was a 'gentleman's agreement in Germany' that no volume performance car should exceed 250km/h (155mph) with a view to increased safety measures on the autobahns following some pretty dire high-speed crashes. The 750i was the first German car to adopt this idea. ASC, or automatic stability control, was an added feature, and the 7 Series was their first model to be fitted with it.

In 1987, just when Vauxhall and Opel were launching the new Senator, a Special Equipment 730i SE cost nearly £25,000 and came fully equipped. This was full of electronic gadgetry and came with an excellent trip computer and left *Autocar* staff with nothing but praise to write about: "... a very competent motor car indeed. It's been five years and £600 million well spent."

The 5-litre 300bhp V12 version from 1987

The centre console of the High Security 733 model.

was identified by its much broader kidney grilles and revised lower spoiler. A long-wheelbase 7 Series also arrived at this time with a handy 4in extra legroom for rear-seat passengers. The extra interior equipment in this executive's car was big.

Furthermore, by adding over 4in to the wheelbase, the 750 iL long wheelbase featured some luxury options: fax machine, a wine cooler and integrated telephone for the busy company director on the move. Xenon high-intensity discharge headlamps were introduced on the 750 iL from 1991 and another key safety feature was added in that the windscreen wipers had increased spring pressure at higher speeds. Another 1991 season model was the V8-powered 740 and iL models, using the same power unit as the E34 5 Series, with power driven through a new ZF five-speed automatic gearbox.

Alpina was on the scene again and offered its B11 3.5 (based on the 740 producing 232kW, but just seven examples were sold. The E32 success story for Alpina was its B12 5.0 based on the 750. The V12 was modified to produce 257kW (up by 3 kW), and around 305 cars were sold. Other special editions from BMW were the 750iL Highline, priced at over twice that of a base 730 model. It was fully loaded. In addition to an already long list of standard equipment items there were:

Cool-box in centre console with two crystal glasses
Leg rests
Independent heating and ventilation
Two batteries and alternators for the extra power drain
Rear-seat radio controls
Electronic and adjustable and heated rear seating
Walnut veneer tables in back of front seats
… and all this for an extra 20,000 DM!

Knocking on the door of the GM Lotus Carlton/Omega supercar, a 304 kW V16-engined derivative was studied by the end of the late 1980s, essentially an enlarged V12 unit coupled to a six-speed manual gearbox borrowed from the E31 8 Series. This was project Goldfisch, or 767. Environmental regulation meant that the superfast model just became a one-off demonstrator. The 'gentleman's agreement' must have been relaxed, as top speed was identical to the aforementioned Lotus Omega at around 175mph, with a 0-60mph time of around 6 seconds.

Production of the E32 continued until 1994 after 311,065 units had been manufactured and when the new fully updated E38 7 Series became available.

E32 7 SERIES BODY TYPES: Five-door saloon. **Manufactured at:** Munich. **Number produced:** 311,065. **Production span:** 1986-1994.
PERFORMANCE (730I SE): Top speed: 131mph/210km/h; **0-60mph/100km/h:** 10.5 seconds; **average economy:** 20-24mpg.

PRICE AT LAUNCH: £24,695 (730i SE).
MEASUREMENTS: Length: 16ft 1¼in (4.91m); **height:** 4ft 7in (1.4m); **width:** 6ft ½in (1.84m); **wheelbase:** 9ft 3½in (2.83m) but add 4½ in (11.4cm) for long-wheelbase version; **kerb weight:** 3792lb (1720kg); **wheels:** 15in; **turning circle:** 38ft 1in (11.9m); **fuel capacity:** 19.8 gallons/90 litres; **boot capacity:** 17.6ft³.
TECHNICAL: Engine types: 3- and 3.5-litre six-cylinder 4-litre V8 and 5-litre V12 petrol; **gearbox:** four-speed manual; **suspension:** independent struts and coils (front), independent coil with anti-roll bar (rear); **brakes:** discs front and rear.
TRIM: Velour, leather, sports steering wheel, anti-theft lock, memory driver's seat.

7 Series (all models) advertising slogans

The BMW 733i. A unique and exceptional choice amongst the world's greatest cars (1978)
BMW will never build a conventional luxury sedan because no one at BMW could bear to drive one (1978)
The BMW 733i. It doesn't scream wealth. It just quietly rewards insight.
The BMW 733i. It reflects the state of your mind, not merely the state of your bank account.
The new BMW special equipment range. Put your mind, not just your body, at ease.
As luxury sedans become more expensive, their inherent worth becomes more critical
The world's most elegant protest against mediocre engineering
1976, 1977, 1978, 1979, 1980. Lap of honour. 1980. Lap of luxury.
A luxury sedan that satisfies both the people who know money and the people who know cars
The luxury car for those who refuse to relax their standards
The luxury car is dead. Long live the luxury car.
You're judged by performance. Why drive a car that lives by a lesser code?
Don't reward a lifetime of achievement with an underachieving car
BMW brings the thrill of performance to the stuffy world of the very expensive luxury sedan
Life is filled with compromises. A $30,000 car shouldn't be.
Every BMW basks in scrutiny that would terrify ordinary cars
For those who know the value of a dollar. A car that justifies spending forty thousand of them.
Why let the year of the car deprive you of the Car of the Year?
He's deciding which car to drive home
Other cars travel the roads. BMWs think their way along them.
BMW is now winning a reputation on circuits like these
It passes Jaguars, Mercedes and petrol pumps
The car that would force its competitors to re-examine their engine technology if they had any
Only the gearbox in this BMW can tell them apart (750iL, 1993)

8 Series E31

The BMW 850, code E31, was produced between February 1990 and May 1999, becoming the first of the 8 Series cars. The other, available from 2018, is not covered in the scope of this book. This model was only available as a two-door coupé, and although not a direct replacement for the earlier 6 Series coupé, it attracted the same customer base, despite being a much higher-performing and enhanced-priced car. Just like the 6 Series coupé, the 850i had slight restrictions when it came to rear-passenger space, and should only be described as being between a full four-seat and a two-plus-two coupé. Powered by normally aspirated V8 (4-litre then 4.4-litre) and a mighty 5-litre V12 petrol engine mated to a six-speed manual gearbox (a first for a V12), design had started in the early 1980s, and its overall design was signed off in 1986. To gauge public reaction, a pre-production prototype was displayed at the Frankfurt Motor Show in September 1989 and received much praise. What was obvious were the much greater aerodynamics of the new coupé, achieving a Cd factor of 0.29 compared with the 0.39 Cd of the 6 Series. The roof structure had no 'B' pillars, which gave the overall impression of a longer, stretched car, and afforded the occupants

A late 1990s 840 Ci with pop-up headlamps, just like the earlier M1.

extra visibility. The front and rear bumpers were integrated into the smooth flow of the body panels, and like the M1 from over ten years earlier, the headlamps were of the pop-up variety, which gave the car a more sporty appearance. Overall it was big – although just under 16ft long, it was almost 6ft in width.

Big engines in big, heavy cars driven by inexperienced motorists can often spell disaster in a fast car. The new ASC+T (automatic stability control plus traction) feature was also adopted for the 850, which gave sharp, drama-free handling and an almost complete lack of wheelspin, as the power to the wheel was cut as soon as it started to lose grip. This facility worked in three modes: by applying a specific brake, by reducing the throttle opening, or by retarding the ignition, all within milliseconds. For the more enthusiastic motorist, this facility could be turned off by way of a switch in the centre console. An option included the dampers adjusting to hard, medium and soft, dependent on the driving style and surfaces encountered. The design of the rear axle meant anti-dive and anti-squat characteristics under heavy braking and acceleration.

Advanced electronics featured heavily inside the cockpit, with full systems-check computer, cruise control, self-lowering windows to aid closure due to air pressure variations, front seats were electrically operated, and screen wipers were vehicle-speed dependent. The steering wheel, seats

The rear aspect of the same 840 Ci. Cars of this era had enormous rear lamp clusters, this being one of the largest fitted by BMW, albeit half of each unit hinged up with the boot lid.

and rear-view mirrors position was memorised for up to three users.

Autocar road tested the 850i in manual form in a September 1991 issue. It praised a fine gearbox, wonderful cabin, effortless power and its general refinement, but was critical of its dull steering, poor economy and "near useless rear seats … only suitable for small children." The £62,727 car achieved a top speed of 159mph, 0-60mph acceleration time of 7.1 seconds but recorded just 14.7mpg overall economy, making the 19.8-gallon fuel tank necessary for the 300-mile range. It was also compared with the 'awesome' Lotus Carlton (Omega) within the test. The automatic version was more thirsty, averaging

The 850i certainly took its rear side window styling cues from the 6 Series coupés.

A 1990 E31 850i.

just 14.4mpg. Earlier in the year the 850 was tested by the magazine against rather ageing, and more expensive competition. It ignominiously won hands down against the Jaguar XJR-S, Ferrari Mondial t and Porsche 928 GT. Plans were made for a high-performance 850, but this never materialised, with the V12 remaining as the flagship of the series.

E31 8 SERIES BODY TYPES: Two-door coupé. **Manufactured at:** Munich. **Number produced:** 30,621. **Production span:** 1990-1999.
PERFORMANCE OF V12: Top speed: 159mph/256km/h; **0-60mph/100km/h:** 7.1 seconds; **average economy:** 15mpg.
PRICE AT LAUNCH: £62,727.
MEASUREMENTS: Length: 15ft 8¼in (4.78m); **height:** 4ft 2½in (1.34m); **width:** 6ft 1in (1.85m); **wheelbase:** 8ft 9½in (2.68m); **kerb weight:** 4149lb (1882kg); **wheels:** 16in alloy; **turning circle:** 37ft 4in (11.5m); **fuel capacity:** 19.8 gallons/90 litres; **boot capacity:** 12.6ft³.
TECHNICAL: Engine types: 4988cc V12-cylinder and 4-litre/4.4-litre V8 petrol; **gearbox:** six-speed manual, four-speed automatic; **suspension:** independent with MacPherson struts and coil springs (front), coil springs and anti-roll bar (rear); **brakes:** ABS with ventilated discs front and rear.
TRIM: Leather.
KEY OPTIONAL EXTRAS: Self-adjusting dampers.

The E31 850i when launched, alongside its sporting forerunners.

8 Series advertising slogans

To a BMW quality inspector, they're identical (316i and 850 Ci)
Butter. Knife (850i, 1997)
It appears there is a limit to BMW genius
Introducing the 5.6-litre, 12-cylinder, 372-horsepower BMW 850 CSi
If a car company can have a soul, this is ours
Pirelli. Once again on the threshold of automotive supremacy
Sehen sie das ganze mal rein wissenschaftlich (Look at it from a purely scientific perspective)
Perfektion aus leidenschaft (Perfection through passion)

1979-1981 – MID-ENGINED M1 (E26)

Toward the mid to late-1970s, the trusty CSL model was reaching the end of its career as a competitive racing car for BMW. A fresh model was needed for competing in the FIA Group 4 racing stable and, so that main production and engineering design was not disrupted, attention turned to Italy. BMW initially worked with Lamborghini, which was at low production at the time and had capacity and experience to produce an all-new mid-engined chassis, and commissioned Ital Design and Giorgetti Giugiaro to design a stunning new body with its powerful 3.5-litre engine mounted mid-ships, a first for BMW copied only once with the i8 hybrid electric in 2012.

Early press picture of the new M1.

The ambitious design brief in the mid-1970s was for a track car that could beat the competition, but was of a high-quality, road-ready format. The resultant beautiful bodywork was extremely up to date, with previous commissions by Giugiaro including the Maserati Merk, Bora and Lotus Esprit, while the later 850i owed its front-end styling influence to the M1. FIA Group 4 homologation regulations dictated that 400 had to be produced over a two-year period, and 454 were manufactured at Stuttgart between 1979 and 1981, with sales of late models continuing until late 1981.

While Lamborghini built four pre-production mules for 900-miles-a-day product testing in 1977, German coachbuilder Baur was responsible for final addition of drive-train components, but final assembled vehicles were sent to BMW Munich for quality testing and any rectifications. Although the model never gained type approval in the UK, a handful of left-hand drive cars made their way into the country. Sadly, as an international racing category, Group 4 racing was at its end by the time the M1 was eventually raced in 1979, following a non-appearance for the 1978 season and resultant cancellation of some customer orders. Indeed, the homologation regulations dictated that the 400 cars not only be built, but sold too, this being the main reason why the 1979 and 1980 Procar one-make series came into being.

The glass-fibre body, using Trasformazione Italiana Resina, was made up of ten panels bonded and rivetted to the multi-tubular Marchesi (of Modena, Italy) chassis/frame

The 160mph M1 was available in the UK from the summer of 1979.

A road-going M1 with its distinctive alloy wheels.

and had a very modern, low squat-style appearance, looking stunning from any angle. Up front were pop-up headlamps surrounding the familiar twin-kidney small front grilles, a long bonnet and steeply raked windscreen. The main beam headlamps were fitted at the corners of the front grille. The cabin doors were wide and rear side windows were small.

Air scoops for engine cooling were evident immediately behind the side quarter windows. The long and full-width rear engine cover (not quite half the length of the entire body) popped up and was hinged at the front for ease of access to the engine. Hydraulic struts held the heavy engine cover up; this included a large, almost horizontal rear screen covered

The Andy Warhol BMW Art M1.

The Andy Warhol car again, photographed from above in 2005.

by horizontal louvres set for rear visibility from the cockpit and, to aid cooling, long side vents were fitted along the base of the sides and eight further vents placed on the top leading edge of the tailgate. Unusually, there was no rear spoiler (save for an uplifted lip at the rear), with this fitment only seen on track examples; however, twin rear, round badges – one at each corner of the hinged panel – left no doubt to car driving behind that this was a special BMW. Also, the Motorsport insignia was fitted to the left of a large M1 motif on the right-hand side.

The earlier idea of using a V10 engine was axed on grounds of cost. Subsequently, power was from a straight-six 3453cc engine of similar format to the later M5 model. The latter's later 1980s marketing made the engine's parentage quite clear. The unit was chain-drive, twin-cam and 24-valve, and a tuned exhaust and unrestricted induction raised the power output from 277 to a whopping 470bhp. Brakes were all servo-assisted large discs of 11.8in (front) and 11.7in (rear) with no anti-lock facility.

Inside the leather-clad, rather sombre grey and black cabin, there was plenty of instrumentation mounted within its own binnacle, but any drivers over six feet tall found it a little restricting, with poor headroom that resulted in a rethink of the seat design by BMW. There was also some criticism of the larger-than-average turning circle – some 42ft! – and the steering was non-power-assisted with 3¼ turns from lock-to-lock. The thick rimmed leather steering allowed for slight adjustment but not for rake, while the pedals were mounted to the right to allow room for wheelarch intrusion. The heating and ventilation controls came from the 3 Series, and a heated rear screen sat immediately behind the occupants, effectively a bulkhead which gave necessary protection from the engine noise.

After early press-launch testing on the continent in the spring of 1978, then a public debut at the Paris Motor Show in October that year, the more comprehensive road testing was eventually performed by UK journalists. *Autocar* magazine got its hands on a red German-registered example as late as October 1980 which achieved 162mph, 0-60mph in 5.5 seconds, and an overall fuel consumption of 17mpg. Handling was described as "leech-like." The speedometer proved to have near-perfect calibration across the speed ranges quoted. Their verdict concluded: "The M1 gives the driver an indefinable feeling of being at one with machine. It was designed to have competition potential (which it clearly has). It happens to have also made a first class road car, possibly the best mid-engined car yet." There was also a comment that it was a shame no right-hand drive cars were to be manufactured.

Main rivals at a similar price, size and performance at the end of the 1970s included the Maserati Khamsin, Aston Martin Vantage, Chevrolet Corvette and De Tomaso Pantera. However, there were production delays after failed dealings with Lamborghini (pilot models had not been delivered on schedule and the company subsequently went into receivership despite the Italian government investing around £1 million to help the M1 project) and heavy overrunning of project budgets. Consequently, BMW Motorsport was put off producing small-run, niche sports projects until the introduction of the Z series and then the i8, and instead turned its attentions to

Formula 1 racing by supplying engines to the Brabham team and producing road-going M3 and M5 models.

Competition M1 models for the track featured flared arches and a front-mounted dam style spoiler, while wider wheels and tyres, and a very substantial rear spoiler, made for a very distinctive look, especially with their bright racing liveries. However, the multi-coloured livery of the Le Mans car of Andy Warhol actually wore off during the 24-hour event! It finished a commendable sixth overall. Starting at the Nürburgring event in May 1979, the M1 was a regular sight in the Procar racing programme that often accompanied F1 events from 1979 and were driven by F1 drivers, with Niki Lauda winning the first title and Nelson Piquet securing the second year. There was no Procar in 1981 after the main sponsor, Goodyear, pulled out of the programme, but the model continued to race at a few events until a Class B victory at the Le Mans 24-Hour in 1984.

E26 M1 SERIES BODY TYPES: Two-door mid-engined coupé. **Manufactured at:** assembled at Ital Design, Italy, with final assembly at Baur, Stuttgart. **Number produced:** 454, of which 397 were road-going. **Production span:** 1979-1981.

There were two BMW roundel badges on the back of the M1, one on each side.

PERFORMANCE: Top speed: 162mph/260km/h; **0-60mph/100km/h:** 5.5 seconds; **average economy:** 15mpg.
PRICE AT LAUNCH: 144,000 DM (around £37,570).
MEASUREMENTS: Length: 14ft 4in (4.36m); **height:** 3ft 9in (1.14m); **width:** 5ft 11¾in

A road-going European M1 in striking red.

(1.82m); **wheelbase:** 7ft ½in (2.56m); **kerb weight:** 3122lb (1416kg); **wheels:** 16in alloy; **turning circle:** 41ft 11in (12.78m); **fuel capacity:** 22.5 gallons/100 litres; **boot capacity:** not quoted, but minimal and at rear.

TECHNICAL: Engine type: 3453cc six-cylinder petrol; **gearbox:** five-speed manual; **suspension:** double wishbone with coil (front), double wishbone with coil (rear); **brakes:** dual-split with discs to front and rear but no ABS.
TRIM: Leather and cloth.

E26 advertising slogans:
Pirellibility (Pirelli tyres advert)
BMW's racing engine is now available to a wider public. But not much wider (with CSL and 635)
The way to drive in the future (with 7 Series)
The evolution of the ultimate driving machine
Six cylinders where you'd expect to find twelve (with 320)
Fate di necessita virtu (virtue of necessity) (with M535i)
Una maccina da Corsa (a racing car) (with 635 CSi)
The latest in a short line of supercars (with CSL and M635)
Il nostro concetto di "6 cilindri" va dalla BMW 320 a ... Le Mans (Our "6-cylinder" concept ranges from the BMW 320 to... Le Mans) (with 320)
Take the M1 to Birmingham
BMW R45: Fangen Sie gleich richtig an (Get started right now) (with motorcycle)
We took the heart out of our racing car... and put it in a new body (with new M535i)

1987-2003 – THE LATER 5 SERIES (E34 & E39)

E34 5 Series

After a five-year design period, the third generation of BMW 5 Series was produced between November 1987 and the end of 1996 not only as a saloon, but a new Touring version – the first estate car seen on a 5 Series platform. Production of this version was from 1992 and lasted until 1996, and all models shared the same 108.7in wheelbase. The E34 was launched universally across the globe in December 1996. Nine different engines were used in the series including petrol and diesel and, following in the footsteps of the 3 Series, the E34 introduced an all-wheel drive model – the 525iX, plus a V8 version.

The 525iX four-wheel drive saloon.

New features included traction control (ASC+T) and stability control (ASC), plus a new six-speed Getrag 420G manual gearbox for the top-range M5 models, but only for its last year of manufacture. Further new electronics included adjustable damping (EDC). The high-performance M5 derivative was made available again and a rather rapid estate Touring model of the M5 also joined the line-up. Alpina was in on the scene again, with the B10 3.0 AllRad, an all-wheel drive with larger engine, the B10 3.5 with a modified engine, the B10 4.0 based on the 4-litre 540i, the B10 4.6 with increased torque and the ultimate Alpina: the 1989-1995 B10 BiTurbo. This car was twice the price of an M5 and competed with Lotus Omega/Carlton from GM, with 507 models made. Make no mistake, this 360bhp car was quick!

There were several models. The entry-level car was the 518i (which just came with manual transmission), which was only available in Europe. Particularly rare is the six-cylinder 325iX, powered by the M50 engine and with rack and pinion steering. Only 9366 such models were manufactured. Two distinctly different 530i cars were built. The 530i grew from a six-cylinder model from 1988 to 1990 to the V8 M60 power for the 1993-1995 model years. The V8 was identified by its wider grille (although this was adopted for other models in 1994) and both versions of the 530i totalled 57,570 in production. The powerful 540i model was added to the range in 1993.

Natural gas and electric E34 prototypes

An E34 'Servicemobile' in Germany displaying all the spares it carried.

An E34 M5 model pleases the crowds.

were also tested. The latter, badged as the 518i EV, was sampled by the Deutsche Post as a potential fleet car. Unlike today's high-voltage EVs, this was 12v and used lead-acid batteries and, through an inverter, drove the rotating-field AC motors. The 518g ran on natural gas and petrol – not unlike the LPG setup, and also shared the concept of less available power when running on gas. The prototype was based on the estate platform, allowing extra room for gas tanks.

The only true limited edition in the E34 range was the 540i LE, which was marketed in the UK and Australia. It had an M5 interior, distinct M-System wheels, self-levelling rear and EDC suspension, its own front air dam and a Servotronic power steering system. Only 70 of these were built and featured an engraved metal plaque placed beneath the handbrake lever on the centre console.

The E34 5 Series was replaced by the E39, although there was some overlap, with the E34 estate version being produced for another six months alongside the new E39.

E34 5 SERIES BODY TYPES: Four-door saloon, five-door estate. **Manufactured at:** Dingolfing (Germany), Rosslyn (Thailand)

An E34 Touring model testing on the skidpan. The model was used on the Allgau Orient Rally in 2017.

and Bangkok (China). **Number produced:** 1,333,412. **Production span:** 1987-1995 (Touring models to 1996).
PERFORMANCE (520I): Top speed: 128mph/205km/h; **0-60mph/100km/h:** 9.5 seconds, **average economy:** 23mpg.
PRICE AT LAUNCH: £17,000.
MEASUREMENTS: Length: 15ft 6in (4.73m); **height:** 4ft 7½in (1.41m); **width:** 5ft 9in (1.75m); **wheelbase:** 9ft ½in (2.76m); **kerb weight:** 3280lb (1490kg); **wheels:** 15in; **turning circle:** 37ft 9in (11.51m); **fuel capacity:** 17.6 gallons/80 litres; **boot capacity:** 16.2ft^3.
TECHNICAL: Engine types: 1796, 1990cc four-cylinder 1991, 2495, 2986, 2997, 3430, 3982, 3535; six-cylinder, 3795cc V8 cylinder petrol; 2443, 2497, 2498cc diesel; **gearbox:** five and six-speed manual; four and five-speed automatic; **suspension:** double-pivot MacPherson struts (front), semi-trailing arms (rear); **brakes:** disc front and rear.
TRIM: Velour, leather.
KEY OPTIONAL EXTRAS: Dual sunroof, headlamp washers, front/rear fog lights, heated front seats, sports seats, leather seats, dipping rear-view mirror.

E34 advertising slogans

Same stable, slightly fewer horses (M5 and 518i compared)
Note the absence of the blue touch paper (M5)
Highly rated by everyone except the tax man (518i)
£16,500 will now open doors you once believed were closed
Now we've added a 4-litre engine, there's even more space behind you (540i Touring)
Unidentified flying object
It's also a neat way to cut service costs (24v models)
The new 8 cylinder 5 Series estate. It'll show most sports cars a clean pair of heels
Tiger without the stripes (Alpina B10 with CSL racer)
Output up. Overheads down. Could this be the businessman's dream? (24v, 1991)
After the bodybuilding comes the brain transplant
"When I was 25, I had one reason to buy a BMW. Now I have three more." (530i Touring)

A 5 Series Touring publicity picture.

E39 5 Series

With design work starting in the early 1990s, and the final body style signed off in 1992, the next development stage took just over three years to complete before the start of production of the fourth-generation 5 Series in 1995: the E39. The Frankfurt Motor Show was the platform used to launch the new (saloon) models, with dealer demonstrator cars available for local test drives at the same time. The new tourer was not produced until the end of the following year, with sales and production of the previous E34 ongoing. For the US market, the estate was known as the Sports Wagon, and such models were equipped with smart roof bars. Available in four-door saloon and soon a five-door estate only, as with its predecessor, a variety of engines were used across the range, including diesels. The highest-performance model was again the M5, and it was the first time it used a V8 engine.

Cars were well equipped, including a new safety feature: curtain airbags that gave head protection in the event of a side collision. Standard fitment across the range included traction control, anti-lock brakes, power steering and pre-tensioners for the front seat belts. A 2001 model facelift occurred in September 2000, with power increases to some engines, the adoption of the M5 kidney grille, revised headlamps and tail lights (these now with LED) and a wide-screen satnav unit (4:3 to 16:9 format). There were various electrical changes from thereon, but outwardly

The B10 Alpina 3.5-litre.

The E39 was replaced by the E60 5 Series in 2003 although, like its predecessor, the Touring models were produced for a further year.

E39 5 SERIES BODY TYPES: Four-door saloon, five-door estate. **Manufactured at:** Dingolfing (Germany), plus CKD kits in Mexico, Indonesia and Russia. **Number produced:** 1,488,038. **Production span:** 1995-2003.
PERFORMANCE (M5): Top speed: 161mph/260km/h; **0-60mph/100km/h:** 5.3 seconds; **average economy:** 16-20mpg.
PRICE AT LAUNCH: £25,765 (520i at in 1997).
MEASUREMENTS: Length: 15ft 8in (4.78m); **height:** 4ft 8½in (1.43m); **width:** 6ft 6in (1.99m); **wheelbase:** 7ft ½in (2.83m); **kerb weight:** 1500lb (3307kg); **wheels:** 15in (18in on M5); **turning circle:** 38ft in (11.6m); **fuel capacity:** 18.5 gallons/70 litres; **boot capacity:** 460 litres.
TECHNICAL: Engine types: 1991, 2171, 2494, 2793 and 2979cc six-cylinder and 3498, 4398

the only major change was the adoption of more brightwork on the boot and body sides.

The long-awaited new M5 was tested by *Autocar* magazine in early 1999. It commented: "The M5 is back with a vengeance. It's been a long wait for this car, but now our patience has been rewarded. Quite simply, the new car is the most impressive high-performance luxury car we've ever driven." Performance was stunning, with 161mph available and a 0-60mph of just 5.3 seconds. The copywriters at the ad agencies were all quick to inform the buying public that "The new M5 can handle 1.2g of lateral force …" and all for £60,000!

The third generation 5 Series in saloon form.

and 4941cc V8 petrol; 1951, 2497 and 2926 diesel; **gearbox:** five and six-speed manual, four and five-speed automatic; **suspension:** independent MacPherson with coils, anti-roll bars (front), multi-link with coils and anti-roll bars (rear); **brakes:** disc front and rear.
TRIM: Velour, leather.
KEY OPTIONAL EXTRAS: Roller sun visors for rear-seat occupants, satellite navigation, boot cover roller blind for the Tourer, latent heat accumulator.

E39 5 Series advertising slogans
'What Car?' Best Executive Car for seven years running
Ample headroom comes as standard
It holds the road like a BMW (540i)
In case you forget what this 140mph vehicle runs on
If you want to go for a spin, choose another car
There is a corner that is forever Munich
Almost perfect
BMW lightweight engineering for natural agility
A more exclusive BMW? Alpina makes it possible
The new M5 can handle 1.2g of lateral force (1999)
And now the real fun begins (Touring)
The biggest change is the one you can't see (2001)

Another new 5 Series, photographed when new in 1995.

The interior of the M5 E39 was certainly both sumptuous and sporty.

The 5 Series Touring arrived in April 1997. This is European specification.

A UK-specification 5 Series Touring.

The comprehensive facia of the new 5 Series.

The rear aspect of a 1999 535i.

The summer 2002 520i ES facelift.

A 528i with Sport Pack.

The 2002 facelifted Tourer model.

1989-2008 – Z1, Z3, Z8 AND Z4 ROADSTERS & COUPÉS

The BMW Z series comprises four series of rear-wheel drive cars produced between 1989 and 2008, all two-door roadsters/ coupé format in front-engine and rear-wheel drive configuration. Many of them have outrageously large engines and commanded a very high new car price. The mechanicals of the Zs were based on the saloon car series of the time, but bodywork was unique for each model. In German, Z stands for Zukunft, which translates to Future. The Z3-based M coupé and M roadster were the first of the Z series to wear the M badge.

Z1

The E30 3 Series was the platform used to base the first of the BMW Z cars on, the Z1. A roadster with a very simple folding MGB-style soft-top made largely of removable and rustless thermoplastic panels, the most distinctive and conversation-provoking feature of this car was its unique doors. An incredible talking piece, to gain entry a remote button is pushed, and the top half of the doors disappear downwards into the sills, followed quickly by the electric window, to allow easy entry. In theory, it could not be driven as such; the doors would have to be placed up again, although the glass could remain down for ventilation. This was for safety reasons in certain markets, but plenty of press photos exist of Z1s at speed with the doors and windows down, and many have been modified to operate as such. The doors work through an ingenious design using electric motors through toothed rubber belts. The car had other unique features such as a roll-hoop integrated into the windscreen top, continuously zinc-welded seams and a flat undertray to further aid in aerodynamics. The 2.5-litre M20 straight-six engine was tilted by 20 degrees to allow for the low hood-line.

The model was unveiled at the Frankfurt Motor Show in September 1987, with production starting over a year later. Just 8000 were built, 6443 of them selling within the German home market, and all examples were left-hand drive, in a range of six bright colours including fun-gelb (fun yellow). There were 3500 ordered after the launch (many from potential investors hoping to make a quick turnaround profit), but demand soon decreased and the model was discontinued in June 1991. In the UK, just over 100 were imported, with around half still on the road. No contemporary magazine advertising was found for this model.

The Z1 with roof deployed, but doors in the up position.

Z1 BODY TYPES: Two-door roadster. **Manufactured at:** Munich. **Number produced:** 8000. **Production span:** 1989-1991.
PERFORMANCE: Top speed: 136mph/220km/h; **0-60mph/100km/h:** 7.9 seconds; **average economy:** 25mpg.
PRICE AT LAUNCH: £83,000 DM (or £26,000).
MEASUREMENTS: Length: 12ft 10¼in (3.92m); **height:** 4ft ½in (1.23m); **width:** 5ft 7in (1.69m); **wheelbase:** 8ft ½in (2.45m); **turning circle:** 33ft 0in (10m); **kerb weight:** 2760lb (1250kg); **wheels:** 15in alloy; **fuel capacity:** 12.75 gallons/58 litres; **boot capacity:** tiny at 9ft^3.
TECHNICAL: Engine types: 2494cc six-cylinder petrol (tilted by 20 degrees); **gearbox:** five-speed Getrag 260/5 manual; **suspension:** MacPherson struts with coils (front), multi-link Z axle (rear), **brakes:** disc front and rear.
TRIM: Leather.

Marco Wittman, BMW Motorsports works driver, shows how good the Z1 doors look when fully down.

A Z1 with both roof and doors down.

Z1 advertising slogans
Heaven to Drive (This was used on a dealer showroom wall poster)
Road Star (This title was used in the sales brochure)
Other than that, the Z1 received very little advertising – it sold itself!

Below: A fine turnout for the 25th anniversary meeting of Z1s at Munich.

Z3 (and M coupé/roadster)

After a three-year break from the Z series, BMW produced the Z3 range between 1995 and 2002. This was the first mass-produced Z-series car, and all were petrol-powered. The two model designations were: roadster (E36/7) and (from 1997) the coupé (E36/8), with the roadster outselling the coupé by about 16 times. The all-enclosed coupé was attractive, however, almost like an estate car looking directly from the rear with more passenger space inside. The sportier M models were introduced in 1998 but only in six-cylinder form. Unusually, this model was not European manufacture, but built in South Carolina.

In 1999, the LCI facelift models entered production. The 2-litre was replaced by a 2.2-litre engine, and the 2.8-litre was replaced by a 3-litre. In the US, the 2.3-litre was replaced by the 2.5-litre. The Z3 was replaced by the Z4 when production ceased in June 2002. Perhaps the best advertising headline was: "Happiness is not around the corner. Happiness is the corner."

A 1999 BMW Z3.

The Z3 interior.

The same 2.0 Z3 from the rear.

The front aspect of the revised Z3 roadster in the summer of 1999.

Distinctive Z3 side vents.

The rear aspect of a silver Z3.

A pristine Z3 at Hunstanton, Norfolk, in 2023.

Z3 BODY TYPES: Two-door roadster and two-door coupé. **Manufactured at:** Greer, South Carolina. **Number produced:** 297,000 (estimated). **Production span:** 1995-2002.
PERFORMANCE: Top speed: 140mph/225km/h; **0-60mph/100km/h:** 6.6 seconds; **average economy:** 23-27mpg.
PRICE AT LAUNCH: £28,350 (1999 2.8).
MEASUREMENTS: Length: 13ft 2¼in (4.05m); **height:** 4ft 3in (1.29m); **width:** 6ft 6½in (1.86m); **wheelbase:** 12ft ½in (2.44m); **kerb weight:** 3200lb (1360kg); **wheels:** 16in alloy; **turning circle:** 33ft 0in (10m); **fuel capacity:** 11½ gallons/51 litres; **boot capacity:** 165 litres (roadster).
TECHNICAL: Engine types: 1.8 and 1.9-litre four-cylinder 2, 2.2, 2.3, 2.5, 2.8 and 3-litre six-cylinder petrol; **Gearbox:** four-speed manual; **suspension:** MacPherson struts, coil springs and anti-roll bars (front), semi-trailing arms, coil springs and anti-roll bars (rear); **brakes:** disc front and rear.
TRIM: Leather.

Z3 advertising slogans
In the Z3, this is your dome light (1999) (shows the open sky and sun)
Twenty years of BMW cars. Most of the memories are blurred (Z3 3.2)
Moments of freedom will never be given to you. You must take them
German beef import (1998)
Happiness is not around the corner. Happiness is the corner
The car is within reach too (2000 and star/space feature)
How could Bond possibly be faithful to just one?
Cloud nine. Cloud ten
Play to win
And, it's safe
You don't have to be small to be agile

Z8 (E52)

The perfect retro-styled front V8-engined rear-wheel-drive roadster? The Z8 was certainly not to be considered as a replacement for the Z3. The more exclusive model overlapped both Z3 and Z4 production and was manufactured between 1998 and 2003 after a five-year development programme. It was originally designed as a tribute to the 1956-1959 507, and the Z07 concept car, which was remarkably similar to the Z8 production car to follow. It was displayed at the Tokyo Motor Show and aroused a lot of interest. On launch, the car cost an incredible $128,000 and, like its 1950s predecessor, power was pure V8.

A colour-matched hardtop was also shipped with every order, and factory parts

The Z8 roadster could be considered a restyled 1950s 507.

availability is ensured for a few more decades to come to ensure any damaged models can continue. One cannot help thinking of the James Bond film *The World is Not Enough* if you are lucky enough to spot one of these rarities, as a silver example was featured in the movie (see TV section at the rear of this book), which is another reason this vehicle is a timeless classic. Just 5703 were built in Munich, with around 45 per cent of these destined for the North American market, up to its demise in 2002. At the end of production, the Alpina Roadster V8 was marketed through the US dealership, the first Alpina to be sold this way. Softer suspension was fitted to this, the ultimate Grand Tourer, and five-speed Steptronic automatic transmission was used and coupled to a 4.8-litre tuned V8 and softer sidewall tyres. Just eight examples were sold in the UK, out of the 555 units produced, most of which went to the US.

Z8 BODY TYPES: Roadster with detachable hardtop. **Manufactured at:** Munich. **Number produced:** 5703. **Production span:** 1998-2002, then Alpina version to 2003.
PERFORMANCE: Top speed: 155mph/km/h; **0-60mph/100km/h:** 4.4 seconds; **average economy:** 20mpg.
PRICE AT LAUNCH: £84,000.
MEASUREMENTS: Length: 14ft 5¼in (4.4m); **height:** 4ft 4in (1.32m); **width:** 6ft 0in (1.83m); **wheelbase:** 8ft 2½in (2.505m); **kerb weight:** 3494lb (1585kg); **wheels:** 18in alloy; **turning circle:** 38ft 9in (11.8m); **fuel capacity:** 16 gallons/73 litres.
TECHNICAL: Engine types: 4941cc V8-cylinder petrol; **gearbox:** six-speed manual; **suspension:** MacPherson struts, coil springs and anti-roll bars (front), independent multi-link, coil springs, anti-roll bar(rear), **brakes:** ventilated discs front and rear.
TRIM: Leather.

Z8 advertising slogans
One careful owner
"It's called a speed limit 007. Try not to break it"
The green mongoose howls at noon

Z9 concept

The little known Z9 GT concept car was exhibited at the Frankfurt Motor Show in 1999 and at Frankfurt Show in Paris. It was a four seater coupé with carbon fibre skin. Inside, it featured a 9in monitor in the middle of the dashboard which housed a central gear lever, push button start and light switches only. Power came from the 3.9-litre V8 turbo-diesel engine of the E38 7 Series. The doors could open in gullwing or conventional fashion.

Z4

Z4 E85/6

The next generation of BMW Z sports car was the first phase of the Z4, the E85 roadster and the E86 coupé. Like its Z3 predecessor,

The Z9 Gran Turismo concept car of 1999.

The new Z4 model from 2002.

the Z4 was manufactured in Greer, South Carolina. It adopted a more angular aggressive look than the Z3, and was produced from July 2002 to December 2008 with a mild facelift in 2006. BMW had announced this car at the Paris Motor Show in 2002, with sales in North America starting in November 2002, while European customers saw their cars from March 2003. As always, power was front-engine and rear-wheel drive, and all but a few earlier cars were fitted with six-speed gearboxes, whether they were automatic or manual. The 3.5-litre used a seven-speed gearbox. There was a choice of five engine types, the largest being a 3.2-litre six-cylinder unit on the M.

Rumoured to have been designed by BMW staff in their own time, the coupé made its debut at the 2005 Frankfurt Motor Show. Like its forerunner the Z3, the coupé looks quite different to the roadster at the rear, but on this later model the rear screen was more steeply raked than the Z3, making it look less like an estate car than the Z3. Internally, there was a little more room in the hardtop compared with the roadster with its soft-top up. Coupés were only available as the 3.0Si and the M-type, and they were a popular choice for circuit racing.

The Z4 was heavier than its predecessor, and to help counteract this, a spare wheel was no longer carried, as the tyres fitted were the run-flat variety, which gave the advantage of a slightly bigger boot space.

A facelifted 'LCI' version was announced at the North American Auto Show in 2006, where new 'si' models joined the range, with revised headlamps, front bumper and tail lights. The Z4 M was also available from 2006. This model represented the sports model of the range, the M designation being used on a Z-badged car for the first time. The Z4 M was manufactured away from the others back on

The side aspect of the Z4.

home turf at the Spartanburg facility in Greer, Germany. Here they fitted hydraulic power steering instead of the electric steering fitted to the others, wider tyres, revised front suspension, a wider front track was used and the brakes and entire rear axle was borrowed from the M3 CSL. These cars were manual only. Of the 5070 Z4 M roadsters built, over half went to the US.

The 168mph Alpina Roadster S (and a Luxury version) were sold in both iterations of the Z4 – pre and post facelift – and could accelerate to 60mph in just over 5 seconds. BMW's plant at Spartanburg sent the bodies to Alpina's facility in Buchloe for building.

The first-generation Z4 production stopped on 28 August 2008, when nearly 198,000 had been produced – 180,856 roadsters 17,094 coupés – to make way for the next Z4, the E89.

The interior of the Z4.

Z4 BODY TYPES: Manufactured at: Greer, South Carolina. **Number produced:** 197,950. **Production span:** 2002-2008. **PERFORMANCE: 2-litre: top speed:** 137mph/220km/h; **0-60mph/100km/h:** 8.2 seconds; **average economy:** 35mpg. **3-litre: top speed:** 155mph (limited); **0-60mph:** 5.5 seconds; **average economy:** 30mpg. **PRICE AT LAUNCH:** £30,000. **MEASUREMENTS: Length:** 13ft 5in (4.09m); **height:** 4ft 3in (1.3m);

Alpina 3.4S Z4.

A UK-spec Z4 looks stunning in black.

The interior of the same black Z4.

width: 5ft 10in (1.78m); **wheelbase:** 8ft 2in (2.495m); **turning circle:** 36ft 1in (11m); **kerb weight:** 3075lb (1395kg), **wheels:** 17 and 19in alloy; **fuel capacity:** 12 gallons/55 litres; **boot capacity:** 10.1ft^3 (coupé) 8.5ft^3 (roadster).

TECHNICAL: Engine types: 1995cc four-cylinder, 2996cc six-cylinder petrol; **gearbox:** five and six-speed manual; **suspension:** struts, coil springs, anti-roll bar (front), multi-link, coil springs, anti-roll bar (rear); **brakes:** disc front and rear.

TRIM: Leather.

A 2003 Z4 corners at speed.

The rear lamps of the 2003 Z4 roadster.

The 2005 Concept Z4 coupé.

The Concept coupé from the front.

The rear aspect of the Z4 M coupé (2006).

A 2006 UK-specification BMW Z4 M coupé.

A 2006 model Z4M roadster.

Z4 advertising slogans

176 bpm (2006)
Evidence that engineering is an art form (2009 model)
The world's fastest soft-top (2003)
Stunning
Built to handle more than a bit of sunshine (Z4 roadster)
Radically thrilling (Z4M coupé, 2006)
Stop playing
It's why we go to work in the morning. It's also why we're early
Land shark (US)
Evidence that engineering is an art form (New Z4, 2009)

The Z4 3.0si SE coupé from 2006.

Z4 – second type (E89)

Although largely outside the scope of this book, the second-generation Z4 was produced from 2009 to August 2016, with its assembly taking place in the newly expanded Regensburg facility in Germany at a cost of 130 million euros. It was launched at the American International Auto Show in Detroit. This model differed in that it had a detachable hardtop, so there was only one body type offered, and this time there was no M-type available.

The 2009 model year Z4, the E89.

1990-2006 – 3 SERIES (E36 & E46)

E36 3 Series (1990-1998)

BMW called the 3 Series "the driver's car since 1975" on some of its early E36 advertising, and this new model did not disappoint. The third generation of the BMW 3 Series was launched initially as a four-door saloon, but this was soon followed by a coupé and a convertible version. All had the new rear Z-axle multi-link suspension system already seen on the Z1 sports car.

A Compact version was available from 1993, known as the 'E36/5'. This model was the first 3 Series to feature a hatchback body style on a shortened overall length. Because of the lack of rear space for the Z-axle multi-link, the E36 Compact used the previous E30's rear semi-trailing arm suspension setup instead. For the E36 3 Series, there was no all-wheel drive iX derivative offered, unlike the previous two series. The touring estate version was not seen until March 1995, with estate sales to this point still being based on the previous E30 platform until as late as 1994. In the US there was a similar line-up of the range, but American customers never saw the smallest 316i or the new four-cylinder diesel cars.

As expected, a performance M3 version was offered from 1993 with 17in wheels and the 3-litre six-cylinder engine, and was capable of 155mph flat out. In 1996, the M3 was fitted with a six-speed manual gearbox. There was no homologation special offered as with previous models that had been developed with a racing career in mind, and M3 specification cars were available in saloon, coupé and convertible configurations. Some journalists complained the whole M3 package appeared way less exciting than its predecessors, and was more like a wide-wheel 325i. The 0-60mph acceleration was impressive, however, at just six seconds.

Alpina was also involved with its specially converted E36 cars. The B6 2.8/2 had an upgraded M50-derived engine, and Japan was exclusive in seeing an estate version of this model. This engine was replaced by a 3-litre and now came in all bodyshell forms,

An advertisement introducing the M3 coupé.

The sleek lines of the cabriolet, this a 3.2-litre M3 from 1997.

Below: The interior of the same M3 cabriolet; a cover for the rear seats (apart from the headrests) with roof down; the steering wheel and facia; and the centre console.

The frontal aspect of the M3 convertible.

The boot badge of the M3.

The M3 model in coupé form, continental specification.

The special interior of a racing 3 Series.

A racing 3 Series cockpit.

E36 M3, rear aspect

with further models using a 3.2-litre engine. However, that was not the end of increased engine sizes as, in 1995 until 1998, the mighty 333hp Alpina B8 was released. A 4.6-litre power unit was fitted, derived from the E34 5 Series mechanicals, and was a very tight fit under the bonnet. Many Alpinas made their way to Japan, including a small number of 4-litre V8 cars. It's not too hard to spot an Alpina, as they all come with their own blue instrumentation panels, their own steering wheel and seats, plus 20-spoke alloy wheels and unique spoilers.

The E36 overlapped with the new E46 available from 1998, with an end production date in 1999. Over 3 million E36s were manufactured worldwide, with production opening up in far-flung corners of the globe, often as CKD kits. The Z3 was another car based on the E36 platform and mechanicals. This model is described elsewhere in this book within the Z section.

The Alpina B3 3.2-litre.

E36 3 SERIES BODY TYPES: Two-door coupé and convertible, four-door Baur convertible, three-door hatchback Compact, four-door saloon, five-door touring estate. **Manufactured at:** Munich, Regensburg (Germany), Rosslyn (South Africa), Greer, South Carolina; CKD: Toluca (Mexico), Jakarta (Indonesia), 6th October City (Egypt), Santa Rosea (Philippines). **Number produced:** 3,042,396 (includes Z3). **Production span:** 1990-1998.
PERFORMANCE (320I SE): Top speed: 132mph/210km/h; **0-60mph/100km/h:** 9 seconds; **average economy:** 25mpg.
PRICE AT LAUNCH: £19,190 (320i SE).
MEASUREMENTS: Length: 14ft 5¼in (4.43m); **height:** 4ft 6in (1.66m); **width:** 5ft 7in (1.71m); **wheelbase:** 8ft 10.3in (2.7m); **kerb weight:** from 2590lb (1175kg); **wheels:** 15in (17in M3); **turning circle:** 28ft 0in (9.4m); **fuel capacity:** 14.3 gallons/65 litres; **boot capacity:** 15.4ft^3.
TECHNICAL: Engine types: 1.6; 1.9; four-cylinder 2.0, 3.2-litre six-cylinder petrol, 1.7-litre four-cylinder, and 2.5-litre six-cylinder diesel; **gearbox:** five and six-speed manual; four and five-speed automatic; **suspension:** MacPherson struts, coil springs, anti-roll bar (front), central control arm with longitudinal and double-track control arms (rear); **brakes:** disc front and rear.
TRIM: Velour, leather.

A publicity photograph of the E36 saloon.

E36 advertising slogans

Pure, undiluted BMW (coupé)
The space race is on again (touring)
Before we put our name to a BMW, we make sure it performs like one (diesel 325 tds)
Until now, that is (328i)
The BMW 3 Series. The driver's car since 1975
Attain perfect peace of mind
It's remarkable what this BMW can hold (touring, 1998)
The space race is on again (3 Series touring, 1995)
Realising the dream (Hartge H3 2.5)
More litres, less gallons (M3 Evolution)
Introducing BMW's Sequential M Gearbox (M3 SMG)
Drawing pin goes here (M3 convertible)
The best-handling car in America. And the seven others that look like they should be (M3 USA)
Heaven above you. Heaven beneath you (M Power)
Oh No (M3)
Not if, which? (whole range)
You've just stolen a moment from life. Allow us to supply the getaway car (M3)
Only a BMW can stop on a pinhead (M3 Evolution)
You wait years for an engine to break 100 bhp per litre. Then two come along together (M3)
The new M3 in yellow. Or incognito

E46 3 Series (1998-2006)

The E46 3 Series was the fourth generation of 3 Series available and was offered in the same five body styles, with press releases announcing the new range published on 11 November 1997. The bodywork was claimed to be 70 per cent more rigid than its predecessor, and an effort was made to reduce the weight of unsprung suspension components by adopting the use of aluminium. Overall, however, when comparing similar models from the ranges, the E46 was around 50kg heavier. All-wheel drive was back again (now Xi or Xd petrol/diesel), having skipped the E36, whereas Valvetronic was a new word for the salesmen, who explained that this was the first 3 Series to have variable valve control on its engine. A facelift programme was released for the 2001 model for the saloons and estates with revised lamps and bumpers.

The shorter Compact models (E46/5) were more easily identified at the front and rear by their unique headlamp and tail lamp designs. These – and what the copywriters dubbed 'rapid-tanning' convertibles – were badged as Ci, and were the first in the series to receive a new steering rack. The coupés and convertibles went through their own facelift for the 2004 model (except for the

The new E46 3 Series saloon.

A new, European-specification E46 3 Series saloon.

M3 versions). Six-speed manual transmission replaced the previous five-speed, revised tail and headlamps, grilles, bonnets and front bumpers.

Faster E46s

The 3.2-litre M3 was released in summer of 2000 as a coupé only, soon followed by the attractive convertible version, both having either six-speed manual or the SMG II automated manual transmission, again with 17in wheels. A faster and lighter CSL (Coupé Sport Lightweight) M3 version was offered, made lighter by use of carbon-fibre panels. For M3s to compete in the American Le Mans Series, ten cars were built and were known as the GTR cars and had Recaro front seats, while the rear ones were removed to gain a weight advantage. Alpina B3 3.3 and B3 S were offered and both were powered by six-cylinder petrol engines. In the US, the ZHP had upgraded camshafts that allowed for an extra 10hp and used a shorter final drive gear ratio.

The result of these upgrades was a vehicle that accelerated from 0-60mph in 5.6 seconds and had a standing quarter-mile timing figure of 14.3 seconds. An attractive Clubsport package was available on 320, 325 and 330 Ci M-sport cars in 2002. The additions included M spoilers, chrome

The E46 3 Series Touring.

The E46 coupé.

exhausts, split rim wheels, door sill badging, half leather upholstery and SMG or Steptronic transmission.

Production of the saloons was discontinued from 2004 when the successor E90 made its debut. In traditional BMW fashion, the coupés, estates and convertibles continued for up to two years.

E46 3 SERIES BODY TYPES: Two-door coupé, three-door hatchback, four-door saloon, two-door cabriolet, five-door estate. **Manufactured at:** Leipzig, Munich, Regensburg (Germany), Rosslyn (South Africa), Shenyang (China), Toluca (Mexico); CKD: Kalingrad (Russia), Jakarta (Indonesia), Shah Alam (Malaysia), 6th October City (Egypt). **Number produced:** 1,918,984. **Production span:** 1998-2006.

PERFORMANCE: Top speed (325i): 144mph/230km/h; **0-60mph/100km/h:** 7 seconds; **average economy:** 26mpg.

PRICE AT LAUNCH (318I): £19,745.

MEASUREMENTS: Length: 14ft 8in (4.47m); **height:** 4ft 7½in (1.41m); **width:** 5ft 8in (1.74m); **wheelbase:** 8ft 11½in (2.72m); **kerb weight:** from 2833lb (1285kg); **wheels:** 15in (17in on M3); **turning circle:** 34ft 6in (10.5m); **fuel capacity:** 13.8 gallons/63 litres; **boot capacity:** 310 litres.

TECHNICAL: Engine types: 1.6 and 2-litre four-cylinder, 2- and 3.2-litre six-cylinder petrol, 2, 2.9 and 3-litre diesel; **gearbox:** six-speed manual, four and five-speed automatic, six-speed SMG II auto/manual on M3; **suspension:** MacPherson struts, coil springs, anti-roll bar (front), Z-axle, coil springs, dampers, anti-roll bar (rear except Compact); **brakes:** disc front and rear.

TRIM: Velour, leather.

A UK-specification early-series E46.

The E46 3 Series coupé, a 1999 model.

The E46 interior – this coupé has the wider doors.

The sumptuous leather interior of the E46 coupé.

The attractive lines of the E46 coupé.

A 2000 3 Series estate at an Alpine ski resort in 2000.

A 2001 M3 coupé with very attractive wheels.

The E46 models had distinctive-shaped headlamps, including this 1999 coupé.

A revised front air dam for the 2002 model year E46, this in touring form.

A slightly earlier convertible with the earlier front air dam.

Below left: European specification M3 convertible.
Below right: Another European convertible, with matching trim colour (1999).

The E46 Alpina saloon.

A 2002 model year 3 Series Touring, UK specification.

By 2004, even diesels were available as convertibles – this is the 320 Cd model.

The M3 CS coupé from 2005.

E46 advertising slogans

Some things should flex. Some shouldn't (convertible)
Advanced car control (328 Ci, 1999)
The new BMW 3 Series and its In Car Entertainment system (318i, 2001)
Pleasure. Distilled (coupé)
It isn't designed to go like the wind (328i SE, 1999)
What was behind this BMW diesel winning the Nürburgring 24-hour race? Every other car (320d, 2000)
After we tune the engine, we tune its sound (330i)
Power. Steering
Rapid tanning (convertible, 2000)
Eye-catching (325 SE Compact, 2002)
Only 422 available in the UK. Being quick has never been so apt. (M3 CSL)
3 Series saloon now with 200% extra (touring)
DNA is responsible for the transmission of hereditary characteristics like strength, agility and looks
The new, more responsive six-cylinder BMW Compact
Yesterday. Today. Tomorrow (323Ci convertible, US)
All-wheel drive, the BMW way. Now available on the 3 Series (US)
What else would you expect from a car designed by a man called Richter? (M3 coupé, 2001)

The 3 Series Compacts were around long before the 1 Series cars, including this 2001 model.

1994-2015 – LATER 7 SERIES (E38, E65, F01)

E38 7 Series 1994-2001

The new 7 Series E38 was the third generation style of 7 Series produced through the late 1990s, and one of the first European cars to be produced with satellite navigation, jointly developed by BMW and Philips. There were three wheelbases available, six petrol engines and three diesels. Various badges were used on these cars: 728, 730, 735, 740, 750 (petrol cars with i or iL suffix) plus 725, 730 and 740 diesels (with tds or d suffix). Gearboxes were either five- or six-speed manual or five-speed automatics. A major styling facelift for the 1999 model included revised front and rear lamp styling, standardising the electronic stability control on all cars and various electrical upgrades.

The long-wheelbase 'iL' was a modest 140mm longer than the standard car, with the extra length gained within the wheelbase and rear doors. There were also bespoke versions of the iL used by government security staff that were offered with an incredible number

An early press photo of the 1997 7 Series.

of options including gun sensors, gas sensors that closed off all ventilation, and extra onboard oxygen in the event of an attack. The very long 'Limousine' wheelbase (250mm longer than the standard iL model), the L7,

The 740iL at Harewood House, UK, and, inset, showing off the fine leather interior. This model was the prestige long-wheelbase car.

A 1997 European-specification 7 Series.

The 1999 750iL.

was for certain markets and used mainly for diplomatic work, and 899 examples were built. They were equipped with a fax machine, a TV, fold-down rear trays, a fridge and electronically controlled rear seats. Later L7s even had rear privacy glass so the chauffeur could not see in the rear. The car's extra length was added between the front and rear doors.

The E38 model was pulled from the North American market in 1997 due to dropping sales, and the 7 Series lasted until 2001 elsewhere, when it gained body-coloured side skirts and clear turn indicators on the run-out models. Overall, 340,242 were produced which, given all the advertising listed below, was quite a low figure, compared to the successful 3 Series and 5 Series.

E38 7 SERIES BODY TYPES: Four-door saloon. **Manufactured at:** Dingolfing, Germany. **Number produced:** 340,242.

Production span: 1994-2001.
PERFORMANCE (730I): Top speed: 140mph/225km/h; **0-60mph/100km/h:** 10.3 seconds; **average economy:** 20mpg.
PRICE AT LAUNCH: £40,895 (730i).
MEASUREMENTS: Length: 16ft 4¼in (4.95m); **height:** 4ft 8in (1.42m); **width:** 6ft 1½in (1.82m); **wheelbase:** 9ft 8½in (2.93m); **kerb weight:** from 3770lb (1710kg); **wheels:** 16in; **turning circle:** 38ft (11.6m); **fuel capacity:** 18.7 gallons/85 litres; **boot capacity:** 0.49m^3.
TECHNICAL: Engine types: 2.8, 3.0, 3.5, 4.0, 4.4, and 5.4-litre six-cylinder petrol, 2.5, 2.9 and 3.9-litre diesel, **gearbox:** five and six-speed manual in certain markets, but mainly five-speed ZF automatic; **suspension:** struts, lower control arms, coil springs, anti-roll bar (front), multi-link axle, track control arms, coil springs, anti-roll bar (rear); **brakes:** disc front and rear.
TRIM: Velour, leather.

The V12 flagship 7 Series of 1999.

E38 advertising slogans

Also equipped for the information superhighway (1995 750iL)
To give you better handling, a BMW is better balanced (1997 740i)
It also steers the car (dashboard and steering wheel)
BMW lightweight engineering for natural agility
We added luxury after luxury and we still couldn't make it boring. You wait years for an engine to break 100bhp per litre. Then two come along together (with M3)
The new M3 in yellow. Or incognito (with M3)
You don't have to be small to be agile (Z3 and 7 Series, 2000)

Revised 7 Series headlamps to match the corporate look from 1999.

7 Series E65 (2001-2008)

The E65 cars were the fourth iteration of the 7 Series range, available between 2001 and 2008 and launched at the Frankfurt Motor Show in September 2001. Again it was available in straight-six petrol and turbo diesel forms, plus in both V8 and V12 petrol power. Transmission was now six-speed across the range. The long wheelbase version was referred to as the E66 and was 140mm longer in the wheelbase, again badged as 'Li'. Overall, the E65 was bigger in all aspects than its predecessor E38, but not that much heavier despite this. Interior and exterior styling was more radical than the previous three 7 Series, adopting a rounder look which certainly kept it looking more modern today. The complicated iDrive infotainment system (hard to use until you get to grips with it) was introduced on this model and, unusually, the centre console was not built tilting towards the driver, as per previous cars. There were many technical introductions to the model, with the key ones being adaptive cruise control, active anti-roll bars, directional headlamps and the E65 was the world's first vehicle to be fitted with an electric parking brake. In 2005, 'automatic high beam assistant' headlamps became available along with 'night vision' with a range of 300m.

Below: A 2001 new E65 7 Series.

An interior view of the E65 long-wheelbase 7 Series.

More high-security models were introduced for the E65 and E66, similar to the E38 specifications, and now BMW offered a buy-back service for the cars for further sale elsewhere, and driver training programmes for owners and chauffeurs keen to learn about emergency situations.

A total of 343,073 E65s were produced, in which 2003 was its most successful year at 57,899 units, overall a similar number to its predecessor. Included in this figure are the CKD completely knocked-down kits assembled as far away as Thailand, Russia and Egypt.

E65 7 SERIES BODY TYPES: Four-door saloon, SWB and LWB. **Manufactured at:**

A 2002 UK 7 Series.

The same model from the side.

Interior appointments for the E65 model.

A UK 745i.

A continental-specification 745i.

the new retooled Dingolfing plant, Germany, and as CKD at Rayong (Thailand), Kaliningrad (Russia) and 6th of October City (Egypt). **Number produced:** 343,073. **Production span:** 2001-2008.
PERFORMANCE (745I): Top speed: 155mph/250km/h; **0-60mph/100km/h:** 6.7 seconds; **average economy:** 20-24mpg.
PRICE AT LAUNCH (745I): £60,000.
MEASUREMENTS: Length: 16ft 6¼in/16ft 11in (5.03/5.17m); **height:** 4ft 10½in (1.49m); **width:** 6ft 3in (1.9m); **wheelbase:** 8ft 3/8ft 7in (2.99/3.13m); **kerb weight:** 4280lb (1945kg); **wheels:** 17in; **turning circle:** 36ft (12.1m); **fuel capacity:** 19.4 gallons/88 litres; **boot capacity:** 500 litres.
TECHNICAL: Engine types: 3.0, 3.6, 4.0, 4.4, 4.8 and 6.0-litre six-cylinder petrol; 3.0, 3.9 six-cylinder and 4.4-litre V8 diesel; **gearbox:** six-speed manual/automatic; **suspension:** struts, coil springs, anti-roll bar (front), multi-link, coil springs and anti-roll bar (rear), **brakes:** disc front and rear.
TRIM: Velour, leather.

E65 advertising slogans
Mirror, signal, outmanoeuvre
Rest assured, the petrol version is just as powerful (730d)
The most powerful diesel in its class (730d)
www.anewwaytodrive.co.uk, NB 89% of companies monitor the time their employees spend on the internet (new 735i, 2002)

7 Series F01

The fifth series of the 7 Series just qualifies to be in the scope of this book, entering after the demise of the E65 in 2008 and lasting until 2015. Identified by a deeper front grille and less cluttered front and rear design that echoes no evidence of a bumper suggestion on its moulding, the F01 (standard wheelbase) and F02 (longer wheelbase) were assembled in Germany, Russia, Thailand, Egypt and India again. Unusually, the model was first launched in Red Square, Moscow, in July 2008, followed by the Paris Motor Show three months later. This time, an all-wheel-drive 7 Series xDrive was on offer from 2009, as was an M Sport package and V12 760iL. There was now an eight-speed automatic transmission, rear-wheel steering, radar cruise control, blind spot monitoring and a lane departure warning system.

Towards the end of F01 production, an ActiveHybrid 7 system could be ordered with the V8 version, with an electric motor mounted into the transmission housing that replaced the alternator and starter. Such models were around 15 per cent more economical on fuel and an extra 140mm was added to the length. Alpina still offered its own upgrades to the 7 Series throughout its run, with a B7 in both pre and post-facelift form. This major facelift occurred for F01 cars in July 2012, when the kidney grille was revised, as was the front spoiler. The following year, rear self-levelling suspension was standardised.

NEW CENTURY SUVS: X5, X3, X6 & X1 (E53, E83, E70, E71 & E84)

X5 E53 & E70

With the X5, BMW ventured into new waters with its North American-built X5 4x4 luxury utility vehicle. Here was a mainstream rival to take on the opposition, including well-established names like Range Rover, Mercedes G Wagon and several Japanese contenders too. Customers familiar with the 5 Series would have noticed that the X5 had incorporated many similar styling features. The E53 was manufactured between 1999 and 2006 at two plants in North America, along with some of the saloons and the Z3, when the E70 took over and continued until the arrival of the third-generation F15 Series. The E53 range was facelifted with a range of new interior colours plus the adoption of new headlights (with corona rings round them like that of the E39), an enlarged and redesigned front grille, updated tail lights, and a redesigned four-wheel-drive system called xDrive. xDrive could vary the power between front and rear axles; instead of the old 62:38 per cent split, power could be sent to exactly

The X5 4.6is from 2002.

where it was needed within a millisecond. Revised engines also gave extra power, with the 4.8is developing 355bhp.

The second-generation X5 was again manufactured in North America, plus now in Russia at Kaliningrad. Also a five-door SUV design, the new model used a similar series of engines as the earlier E53, but transmission was limited to either six-speed Steptronic or eight-speed ZF automatic formats. Styling was more conservative but with a slightly longer 2933mm wheelbase, plus a wider and longer body, just right for those North American highways. The well-established xDrive four-wheel-drive transmission was continued on in this model, but a new feature – which was being adopted by other mainstream manufacturers such as Peugeot – was a

The X5 SUV was certainly a game-changer for BMW.

A 2003 X3 3.0i.

panoramic glass roof. The extra length meant that, at last, the X5 could be ordered with a third row of seats fitted at the rear, and the interior was completely refreshed.

Introduced at the New York Motor Show in 2009, a sporting E70 X5M was built between 2010 and 2013, to compete with top 4x4 models from Jeep, Porsche and Mercedes. Up to 547bhp was on tap from its TwinPower Turbo V8 engine. This heavy car could outsprint most conventional cars, with an incredible 0-60mph time of just four seconds, and various TV shows and magazines were keen to try out this new model. It had just about the biggest disc brakes ever fitted to a BMW production car and came complete with its own uprated suspension and wider wings, plus traction control. Facelifted LCI E70s were launched in 2010 and included revised bumpers, tail lights, headlamps and grilles, adopting the much loved BMW corporate look.

The X5 high-performance model (2000).

A standard-specification X5 in 2000.

There was also an increased range of interior and exterior colours.

E53/E70 (MK1 AND 2) X5 BODY TYPES: Five-door estate. **Manufactured at:** Spartanburg (US) and Toluca (Mexico). **Number produced:** 560,000 (E53) and 700,000 (E70). **Production span:** 1999-2006, then 2006-2013.
PERFORMANCE (3.0I PETROL): Top speed: 126mph/200km/h; 0-60mph/100km/h: 8.8 seconds; **average economy:** 18mpg.
PRICE AT LAUNCH: £33,000 (entry-level model in 2001).
MEASUREMENTS (E53): Length: 15ft 3¼in (4.66m); **height:** 5ft 8in (1.71m); **width:** 6ft 1in (1.87m); **wheelbase:** 9ft 3in (2.82m); **kerb weight:** 4640lb (2090kg); **wheels:** 19in; **turning circle:** 39ft 4in (12.1m); **fuel capacity:** 20 gallons/92 litres; **boot capacity:** 465/1550 litres (seats up/down).
TECHNICAL: **Engine types:** 3.0, (later) 3.5-litre six-cylinder, 4.4, 4.6 and 4.8, (and later) 5.0-litre V8 petrol; 2.9 and 3-litre six-cylinder diesel; **gearbox:** five and six-speed manual and six-speed automatic all 4x4; **suspension:** MacPherson struts, roll bar, coil springs (front), multi-link semi trailing arms, coil springs and anti-roll bar (rear); **brakes:** disc front and rear.
TRIM: Cloth, leather.
KEY OPTIONAL EXTRAS: Third row of seats (E70), soft-close boot feature, trailer stability programme and adaptive headlamps. A security version with ballistic protection was also offered.

X5 advertising slogans
Downhill (2000)
Agility (2001)
Dynamic handling (2002)
xDrive transfers power to / needed most / where it is (X5, 2004)
Our designers got the seven-year itch. And scratch they did (2007)

X3 E83

So far, there have been four generations of the X5 SUV utility vehicle, including those outside the scope of this book:

E83 – 2003-2010
F25 – 2010-2017
G01 – 2017-2024
G45 – 2024 on

The E83 X3 first-generation was based on the 3 Series platform, and was designed in conjunction with Graz and largely built in its production plant in Austria. The model made its debut at the Frankfurt Motor Show in September 2003, and featured the new

A 2006 X3.

A 2006 X3 again, side profile.

xDrive all-wheel-drive system, later adopted for other 4x4s in the BMW range. This system allowed instant torque to either axle, which was normally fed 40 per cent (rear) and 60 per cent (front). Overall, it weighed around 10 per cent less than the existing X5 with a smaller footprint but a similar height. The vehicle won 'Canadian Car of the Year' for best sports utility in 2005, a year in which the Bluetooth facility could be built in to order by the factory, but in reality, it hardly ever worked despite continued efforts by local service engineers. 2006 US models could be ordered with the full M body kit plus panoramic glass roofs and adaptive headlamps. This package was replaced in March 2009 by the Sport Line Limited Edition. A facelift was announced to the X3 in September 2006, with revised bumpers, interior trim, suspension and engines.

E83 X3 BODY TYPES: Five-door estate. **Manufactured at:** Graz (Austria), Rayong (Thailand), 6th October City (Egypt), Kaliningrad (Russia). **Number produced:** 614,000. **Production span:** 2003-2010.
PERFORMANCE (2.5l): Top speed: 130mph/210km/h; **0-60mph/100km/h:** 8.9 seconds; **average economy:** 27mpg.
PRICE AT LAUNCH: £28,715 (2.5i SE in 2004).
MEASUREMENTS: Length: 14ft 11¼in (4.56m); **height:** 5ft 6in (1.63m); **width:** 6ft 1in (1.85m); **wheelbase:** 10ft 0in (2.79m); **kerb weight:** 3084lb (1840kg); **wheels:** 17in; **turning circle:** 32ft 2in (11.7m); **fuel capacity:** 15 gallons/67 litres; **boot capacity:** 480 litres.
TECHNICAL: Engine types: 2.0 four-cylinder; 2.5 and 3.0 six-cylinder petrol; 2.0 four-cylinder; 3.0 six-cylinder diesel; **gearbox:** six-speed manual or automatic; **suspension:** double wishbone, roll bar, coil springs (front), multi-link semi trailing arms, coil springs and anti-roll bar (rear); **brakes:** disc front and rear.
TRIM: Cloth, leather.
KEY OPTIONAL EXTRAS: Park distance and rear-view camera.

X3 advertising slogans
Introducing the new BMW X3 with xDrive (2004)
Where will you go next? (2006)
Joy is everything you'd expect from a 4x4, and less (2010)

The stylish interior of the 2006 X3.

The crossover X6 sports utility 4x4.

X6 E71

Although verging on the end of this book's cut-off date, the E71 was the first of a generation of X6 crossover models and was produced as follows:

E71 – 2007-2014
F16 – 2015-2020
G06 – 2020-present

Its quirky crossover appearance was notably different to the more upright X5 and X3 cars, with production split between the US and Russia. The term 'crossover' refers to a combination of 4x4, hatchback design yet the appearance of a sports coupé. A high boot lid, with pronounced rear wheelarches keeps the X6 from looking dowdy at the rear, especially with such a strong aggressive front end. Power availability was, again, across diesel and petrol engines. The 547bhp X6 M model was produced from April 2009 and featured some interesting features such as four-piston calliper front brakes, aluminium pull-style paddles mounted on the steering wheel, lower Adaptive Drive suspension, wider 20in wheels with run-flat tyres, hill descent and dynamic stability controls. M performance parts that could be ordered included a black kidney grille, M-style wheel rims, sports steering wheel and a carbon-fibre spoiler.

An active hybrid version of the X6 made its debut at the Frankfurt Motor Show in 2009, allowing drivers to use standard internal combustion power, just electric, or

The M sport edition of the crossover X6 from 2014.

a combination of both, allowing for greater acceleration. X6 models up to 2012 were only available with four seats. *Autocar* magazine concluded on its June 2008 road test: "Does the world really need a car with such large external dimensions that has such limited interior space?" However, the test was very favourable, despite the car's heavy thirst for fuel.

E71 X6 BODY TYPES: Five-door crossover. **Manufactured at:** Greer (US), Kaliningrad (Russia). **Number produced:** 265,000. **Production span:** 2008-2014. **PERFORMANCE: Top speed:** 147mph/235km/h; **0-60mph/100km/h:** 7.5 seconds; **average economy:** 26-30mpg. **PRICE AT LAUNCH:** £44,145. **MEASUREMENTS: Length:** 16ft in (4.87m); **height:** 5ft 6½in (1.68m); **width:** 6ft 6in (1.98m); **wheelbase:** 9ft 6in (2.93m); **kerb weight:** 4850lb (2185kg); **wheels:**

20in; **turning circle:** 35ft 3in (12.8m); **fuel capacity:** 19 gallons/85 litres; **boot capacity:** 570/1450 litres (seats up/down).
TECHNICAL: Engine types: 3.0-litre six-cylinder, 4.4-litre V8 petrol, 3.0-litre six-cylinder, 4.4-litre V8 diesel; **gearbox:** six, seven and eight-speed automatic; **suspension:** double wishbones, coil springs and anti-roll bar (front), multi-link, coil springs and anti-roll bar (rear); **brakes:** ventilated disc front and rear.
TRIM: Leather.

E71 X6 advertising slogans
Taking the coupé into uncharted territory (2008)
A coupé above (US)

X1 (E84)

The E84 was the first of a generation of three entry-level SUV X1 cars as follows:

E84 – 2009-2015
F48/F49 – 2016-2022
U11/U12 – 2022-present

The debut of the X12 was the Concept X1 shown at the Paris Motor Show in October 2008. Production models used the same E90 3 Series platform and wheelbase (2760mm) and it was labelled as a sub-compact crossover model. It was built across the globe as a cheaper rear-wheel-drive-only version for drivers not wanting the extra terrain capability. The sDrive complemented the xDrive 4x4. BMW had stated the X1 was built for a very wide customer base and it was certainly priced competitively. On a 2011 triple road test between the new Range Rover Evoque, an Infiniti EX30d and a X1 23D SE, *Autocar* magazine found the X1 the "most enjoyable on a point-to-point drive" but also stated "A sense of functionality dominates the X1's somewhat plain interior."

A facelift occurred in 2012 and was first publicly seen at the New York Motor Show that year. It included refreshed lights all round, new mirrors that included the indicators and a revised front bumper. Internally, there was a new centre console design, revised steering wheel plus new interior trim options. An interesting urban explorer model first seen at the 2012 Los Angeles International Auto Show was the Powder Ride edition for the larger-engined cars. Apart from exclusive paint colours, there were 18in wheels, roof rack and box and bespoke decals.

E84 X1 BODY TYPES: Five-door compact crossover. **Manufactured at:** Leipzig

A continental X1 made an interesting entry-level SUV for BMW.

The E84 X1.

(Germany), Shenyang (China), Chennai (India), Jakarta (Indonesia), Rayong (Thailand), Kulim (Malaysia), Kaliningrad (Russia) and Araquari (Brazil). **Number produced:** 820,000. **Production span:** 2009-2015.
PERFORMANCE: Top speed: 127mph/205km/h; **0-60mph/100km/h:** 7.2 seconds; **average economy:** 40mpg.
PRICE AT LAUNCH: £22,660 (sDrive 18d SE); £29,055 (xDrive 23d SE).
MEASUREMENTS: Length: 14ft 7¼in (4.45m); **height:** 6ft ½in (1.54m); **width:** 6ft 10in (1.78m); **wheelbase:** 9ft ½in (2.76m); **kerb weight:** 3153lb (1430kg); **wheels:** 17 and 18in; **fuel capacity:** 13.4 gallons/61 litres; **boot capacity:** 14.8ft^3 (420 litres), seats up; 47.7ft^3 (1350 litres) seats down.
TECHNICAL: Engine types: 1.6, 1.8, 2.0, 2.8-litre four-cylinder; 3.0-litre six-cylinder; petrol and 1.6, 1.8, 2.0-litre four-cylinder diesel; **gearbox:** six-speed manual or eight-speed automatic; **suspension:** MacPherson struts, coils, (front), coils (rear), **brakes:** disc front and rear.
TRIM: Leather.

X1 advertising slogans
Joy follows its heart; not the GPS (2009)
Adventure is waiting (2016)
Get back to driving. The new BMW X1 (2012)

The X1 shows its potential urban explorer possibilities with an optional bike rack.

2003-2010 – 5 SERIES & 6 SERIES (E60/61 & E63/64)

E60/61 5 Series

Back in 1997, design and development was started on the E60, the fifth generation of 5 Series. Saloon production started in July 2003 and estate cars in May 2004. The 5 Series rolled off eight production lines across the world until 2010, six of them built from completely knocked-down kits (CKD). Bodywork was available in a four-door saloon, a longer-wheelbase saloon (for China, built at their Brilliance production facility) and an estate touring version. As with previous models, power was available in either petrol or diesel through a variety of engines of straight-four, straight-six, V8 and V10 configuration. All models were either manual or automatic six-speed configuration, except for the V10-powered M5, which used the SMG auto/manual seven-speed gearbox.

Life Cycle Impulse (LCI) facelifted models made their debut in early 2007, receiving restyled, adaptive headlamps, plus subtle changes to the tail lights, and a new-style front bumper that had changes to the air intake area. Engines were upgraded to match those used in the new X5. Internal revisions were plentiful, including a complete upgrade to the iDrive system, and shift paddles were now used on the saloons in addition to the M5, as was the case previously. The previous mechanically operated automatic gearbox was replaced by the shift-by-wire mechanism from this point.

Top models

The 500bhp V10 M5 was the top BMW-badged model, and was the world's first production V10 car. It was available in saloon and estate form in Europe; 20,548 were produced, with a production ratio of 19:1 compared with the tourer version. Performance, as always, was spectacular, with a 0-60mph time of just 4.7 seconds, now Tesla territory. A sequential manual gearbox (SMG) was used with paddle shifts on the steering wheel. The E63 and E64 M6 coupé was based on the M5 chassis, and was available from 2004 to 2019. From February 2005, Alpina built its own 493bhp B5 and 523bhp B5S (in saloon and estate) models, both with the 4.4-litre V8s with their additional centrifugal superchargers.

Overall, a total of 1,369,814 5 Series were built in relatively similar numbers for each year of production (1,096,444 E60 saloons and 263,426 E61 estates), with the last leaving production lines in 2010 with the forthcoming F10 5 Series due to take over.

E60/61 5 SERIES BODY TYPES: Four-door saloon plus five-door estate. **Manufactured at:** Germany, China, plus CKD in Russia, Egypt, Indonesia, Mexico, Thailand and India. **Number produced:** 1,369,814 including 20,548 M5s. **Production span:** 2003-2009.

The new M5 from 2004.

A 2010 UK police 5 Series.

PERFORMANCE: Top speed: 155mph/250km/h; **0-60mph/100km/h:** 5.8 seconds; **average economy:** 20-30mpg.
PRICE AT LAUNCH: £25,850 (520i SE).
MEASUREMENTS: Length: 15ft 10¼in (4.84m) – Chinese LWB is 5½ longer; **height:** 4ft 10½in (1.47m); **width:** 6ft 1in (1.85m); **wheelbase:** 9ft 5½in (2.89m); **kerb weight:** from 3406lb (1545kg); **wheels:** 17in; **turning circle:** 34ft 2in (11.4m); **fuel capacity:** 18.5 gallons/70 litres; **boot capacity:** 560 litres.
TECHNICAL: Engine types: 2.0-litre four-cylinder, 2.2, 2.5 and 3-litre six-cylinder, 4.0, 4.4 and 4.8-litre V8, 5.0-litre V10 petrol; **gearbox:** six-speed manual or automatic (M5 automatic seven-speed), **suspension:** (front), (rear); **brakes:** disc front and rear.
TRIM: Velour, leather.

E60 advertising slogans

Quietly overstated (M sport 2005)
The new BMW 5 Series with a head-up display allows you to receive vital information without having to look down
Active steering. You don't need it, like you didn't need a mobile phone
Dynamic driving evolves to a new level (Australian)
Bigger boots. More well. (touring)
From a family of sports cars… a family sports car (5 Series touring, 2004)
Excitement and Economy. Exclusive and Affordable (Alpina D3, 2006)
The first of its kind (new 5 Series Gran Turismo in 2009)

A 520d from 2007.

The 2007 M5 Touring was a very capable long-distance estate car. Note its pair of twin exhausts.

M6

The top model of the E63 and E64 was the M6 from 2005 (coupé) and 2006 (convertible). The M6 sold 14,152, made up of 9087 coupés and 5065 convertibles.

E63/64 6 Series

Unveiled at the Frankfurt Motor Show in 2003, the E63 6 Series coupé brought back a name last used in the 1980s, and again it represented the biggest BMW coupé available. The E64 convertible version of the 6 Series was unveiled at the Detroit Motor Show in early 2004 and released that summer. The mechanicals and chassis of both models were largely based on the E60 5 Series, but unlike in the 1970s/80s, a 3-litre diesel version was offered from 2007 on with the new mildly facelifted models. Overall, the wheelbase was around 4in shorter than the E60. The E63 range was replaced by the F12 and F13 ranges in 2012.

E63/64 6 SERIES BODY TYPES: Two-door coupé and two-door convertible. **Manufactured at:** Dingolfing (Germany). **Number produced:** 116,748 (62,575 coupés and 54,173 convertibles). **Production span:** 2003-2010.

PERFORMANCE: Top speed: 155mph/250km/h; **0-60mph/100km/h:** 5.4 seconds; **average economy:** 22-30mpg.

PRICE AT LAUNCH: £45,255.

MEASUREMENTS: Length: 15ft 10in (4.82m); **height:** 4ft 6in (1.37m); **width:** 6ft 1in (1.85m); **wheelbase:** 9ft 1½in (2.78m); **kerb weight:** 3280-4250lb (1490-1930kg); **wheels:** 18in; **turning circle:** 41ft 0in (12.5m); **fuel capacity:** 15.4 gallons/70 litres; **boot capacity:** 15.9ft^3.

TECHNICAL: Engine types: 3.0-litre six-cylinder, 4.4 and 4.8-litre V8, 5.0-litre V10

The 6 Series coupé of summer 2003.

The Alpina 6 Series coupé.

petrol, 3.0-litre six-cylinder turbocharged diesel; **gearbox:** six-speed manual and automatic, seven-speed SMG; **suspension:** independent, double wishbones, coil springs (front), independent double wishbones (rear); **brakes:** vented disc front and rear.
TRIM: Leather.

E63 E64 advertising slogans

You've spent your whole life on the waiting list (E63)

Performance Without Sacrifice (US – E63, E64)

U.O.U. (US – convertible)

2004-2013 – SMALL/ COMPACT CARS: E87 1 SERIES & E90 3 SERIES

E87 1 Series

The name 'Compact' had already been used for the shorter hatchback versions of the 3 Series since the mid-1990s. The new E87 BMW 1 Series were the new entry-level compact cars for BMW from 2004, first seen at the Paris Motor Show in September that year as five-door hatchbacks, although they were not specifically badged as compacts. Subsequent 3 Series models introduced no longer supported the Compact name. By 2007, conventional three- and five-door hatchbacks, plus two-door coupés and convertible models were produced all on the same 104.7in (2.66m) wheelbase, and all following the tradition of BMW's rear-wheel drive, unlike most of the competition at this price point and physical size.

The E designations used for the 1 Series, and their production dates, were:

E81	three-door hatchback	July 2007-2012
E82	coupé	Nov 2007-Aug 2013
E87	five-door hatchback	Sept 2004-2011
E88	convertible	2007-June 2013

The cheapest BMW 1 Series for the 2005 model – only produced as a five-door hatchback – was the £15,690 116i, and the most expensive the 120d SE at £20,800. Initially there were limited model specifications, with the base 'i' model, SE and Sport in both petrol and diesel power. The flagship of the range, the turbocharged M coupé, followed later, along with non-M-specification 3-litre cars, the 135i models, which only made their way to the North American market in 2013. The E87 Series was replaced in 2011 by the second 1 Series, the F20/F21, although the E82 coupé and E88 convertible remained in production until 2013. Its best year of production was 2008, when 225,095 1 Series were manufactured, equating to about one fifth of BMW production overall.

Towards the end of production, when all four body types were still available, the UK retail prices were as follows in November 2012. Prices are for the top-specification model for each body style:

135i M	£29,995	three-door hatchback
135i M	£30,525	five-door hatchback
135i M Sport	£32,150	two-door coupé
135i M Sport	£35,795	convertible

In all, over 1.5 million 1 Series Compact cars were produced over six years, although the coupe and convertible models continued on for another two years.

E87 E81 E82 E88 1 SERIES BODY TYPES: Two-door coupé and convertible, three and five-door hatchback. **Manufactured at:** Leipzig and Regensburg, Germany. **Number produced:** 1,547,751. **Production span:** 2004-2013. **PERFORMANCE (M COUPÉ):** **Top speed:** 155mph/250km/h; **0-60mph/100km/h:** 4.6 seconds;

The 2004 1 Series all had short rear overhangs. This is the 120d. The side aspect shows the smaller boot capacity of the Compact models very well.

Above: UK-specification 1 Series Compact in 2004.

Left: The rear aspect of a 1 Series seen in Monte Carlo.

The internal appointments of the 1 Series entry model.

average economy: 25-30mpg.

PRICE AT LAUNCH: £15,690 (116i).

MEASUREMENTS: Length: 13ft 10¼in (4.23m); **height:** 4ft 8in (1.42m); **width:** 5ft 9in (1.75m); **wheelbase:** 8ft 6in (2.66m); **kerb weight:** 2015lb (1385kg); **wheels:** 17 and 18in; **turning circle:** 35ft 10in (10.9m); **fuel capacity:** 11½ gallons/52 litres; **boot capacity:** 370 litres (coupé), 360 litres or 1200 litres (hatchback seats up or down).

TECHNICAL: Engine types: 1.6, 2.0-litre four-cylinder, 3.0-litre six-cylinder, petrol, 2.0-litre four-cylinder diesel; **gearbox:** five then six-speed manual and six and eight-speed automatic, **suspension:** MacPherson struts, coil springs, anti-roll bar (front), multi-link, coil springs, anti-roll bar (rear), **brakes:** ventilated disc front and rear.

TRIM: Velour, leather.

KEY OPTIONAL EXTRAS: Driver comfort pack, folding mirrors.

E87 E81 E82 E88 advertising slogans

Makes you want to get behind the wheel (E82)

Bringing summer to every street (convertible, US)

One origin. Two originals

The 2007 1 Series M Sport.

The 135i Coupé, 3-litre. The twin-turbo engine won International Engine of the Year in 2007 and 2008, judged by a panel of 65 automotive journalists from 32 countries.

The 1 Series M Coupé from 2009 – a very rapid coupé.

The M Coupé from the rear.

E90 3 Series

The E90 3 Series was available from 2005 to 2012 and superseded the earlier and slightly smaller E46 Series. Initially just a four-door saloon and five-door estate version were offered from March 2005, followed by a coupé in 2006, and finally the convertible in 2007. As always, petrol, diesel, manual and automatics, plus all-wheel-drive cars, were among the line-up. Australia never received any all-wheel-drive (X-Drive) E90 cars.

The LCI facelift for the saloon and estate occurred in September 2008. There were many small detail enhancements, but the most noticeable were the restyled bumpers at each end, and wider kidney grilles. The wing mirrors, boot lids, headlamps and tail lights all had a makeover, too.

The E series designations were:

E90 saloon (four-door)	Dec 2004-Oct 2011
E91 estate (five-door)	Sept 2005-May 2012
E92 coupé	June 2006-2013
E93 convertible	Dec 2006-Oct 2013

The E91 estate model, badged as Touring in Europe and Sports Wagon in the US, was less common for continental markets, with Australia only receiving a small number. The M3 was never produced as an estate. The most sporting estate would have been the M

A police-specification 330d 'saloon interceptor'.

Sport specification, this option being available across the whole range. The strictly four-seat-only coupé was identified at the rear by its distinctive L-shaped rear lights, restyled headlamps and smaller side windows that set it apart from the other models. Being on a two-door frameless window platform, the side doors were longer than those of the saloon and estate cars. Just like the old pillarless 1980s SEC Mercedes coupés, the front seat belt stalks were mounted on motorised arms that extended forward to harness in the front passengers from their B-post locations. These were the last of the 3 Series coupés (and convertibles); the next F32 and F33 generation would be called the 4 Series.

The convertible broke new ground for the E90 models. Long gone was the less-than-secure fabric roof fitted on so many convertibles in the past. The open-top BMW

A new 2004 German-registered 3 Series from the rear.

The 2007 model M3 Coupé (E90).

3 Series now came with a retractable folding metal roof (not unlike the Volkswagen EOS), and remote deployment was electric and activated by the key fob. There was a 38 per cent gain in visibility and, of course, better structural rigidity over the soft-top convertibles without the roof down.

M3 and Alpina

At the top of the E90 series stable was the mighty 4-litre V8 models available in saloon, coupé and the now more rigid convertible bases. By 2009 prices were £49,900 for the saloon, £51,330 for the coupé and £55,300 for the electric-roof convertible. In May of 2011, *Autocar* magazine pitched the M3 coupé M-DCT against the Mercedes C63 AMG coupé, a natural rival. Both V8s were confirmed to have the commonly European-adopted restricted top speed of 155mph, with the Mercedes just ahead in the 0-60mph acceleration times (4.4 v 4.6 seconds). Despite this slight advantage, the testers concluded: "BMW's perennial king of performance coupé is still on its throne". On the handling, one member of staff mentioned "I can't help feeling that the M3 driver must be having more fun." The Alpina models were based on any of the four platforms built, with the B3 having turbocharged six-cylinder petrol power, and the D3 powered by a turbocharged four-cylinder diesel engine.

3 SERIES E90 BODY TYPES: Two-door convertible and coupé, four-door saloon and five-door estate. **Manufactured at:** Leipzig, Munich and Regensburg (Germany), Rosslyn (South Africa), Shenyang (China), Toluca (Mexico), 6th October City (Egypt), Rayong (Thailand), Jakarta (Indonesia), Kulim, Kedah (Malaysia), Kaliningrad (Russia). **Number produced:** 3,076,085 including 1,825,549 saloons. **Production span:** 2004-2013.
PERFORMANCE: Top speed (330d M Sport): 155mph/250 km/h; **0-60mph/100km/h:** 6 seconds; **average economy:** 40mpg.
PRICE AT LAUNCH: £19,450 (316i).
MEASUREMENTS: Length: 14ft 10in (4.52m); **height:** 4ft 6½in (1.38m); **width:** 5ft 10in (1.78m); **wheelbase:** 9ft ½in (2.76m); **kerb weight:** 3607lb (1625kg); **wheels:** 16-20in; **turning circle:** 33ft 0in (11m); **fuel capacity:** 13.5 gallons/61 litres; **boot capacity:** 460 litres.
TECHNICAL: Engine types: 1.6, 2-litre four-cylinder, 2.5, 3-litre six-cylinder, 4-litre V8 petrol, 2-litre four-cylinder, 3-litre (six-cylinder) diesel; **gearbox:** five and six-speed manual,

It was always a treat to see the now-hardtop electric roof deployment on the M3 convertible (2008 photo).

six-speed automatic, seven-speed dual clutch; **suspension:** MacPherson struts, coil springs, anti-roll bar (front), multi-link, coil springs, anti-roll bar (rear), **brakes:** disc front and rear.
TRIM: Velour, leather.

KEY OPTIONAL EXTRAS: Premium Package, Cold Weather Package, Sports Package, Technology Package and the Performance Power Kit.

E90 advertising slogans
Joy does not compromise. Joy is futureproof (320d ED, 2010)
You'll find it hard to pass (3 Series Coupé Sport, 2011)

THE FUTURE'S ELECTRIC – i3 & i8

Battery-powered cars had been around ever since the turn of the last century, until petroleum spirit was available from chemists and then roadside garages, then internal combustion cars really took off, negating the need to charge the DC voltage batteries that then gave a very limited range. There are several completely different prototypes discussed below, but the first two production electric BMWs were the i3 fivew-door hatch and the sporting two-door i8. Both of these cars were of the same modern design, using carbon-fibre body frame and some panels, with plastic panels bolted to this. They were marketed under the BMW I sub-brand.

It is important to point out that BMW had produced various electric prototypes towards the end of the last century, most notably the 1602 electric in 1972, and the all-new-bodied three-door E1 Z11 city car in 1991 and shown at the Frankfurt Motor Show. Some other models also had electric derivatives running as test mules and were often tested by such companies as the German Post Office for viability studies. With the E1, bodywork was sub-compact in size and very attractive, much in keeping with the rest of the BMW range.

The early 1970s 1602 silent electric was hard to spot from the rear – except for the lack of an exhaust.

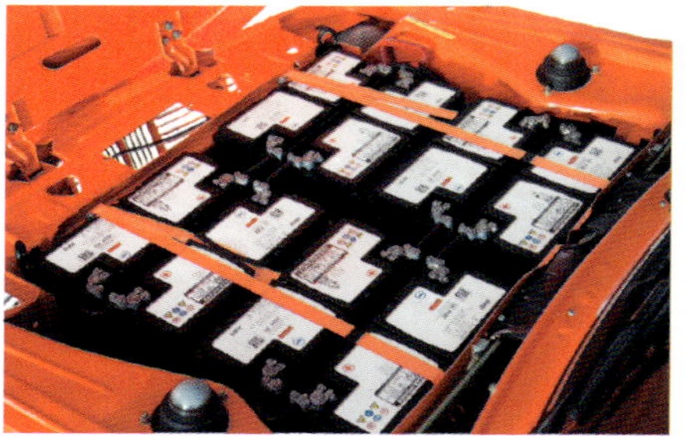

The 16 12v battery line-up under the bonnet of the 1602 Elektra.

A cutaway illustration of the electric power layout of the 1602 with electric drive.

An early prototype picture of the E1 electric car study.

Several E1s were up and running, usually in bright colours.

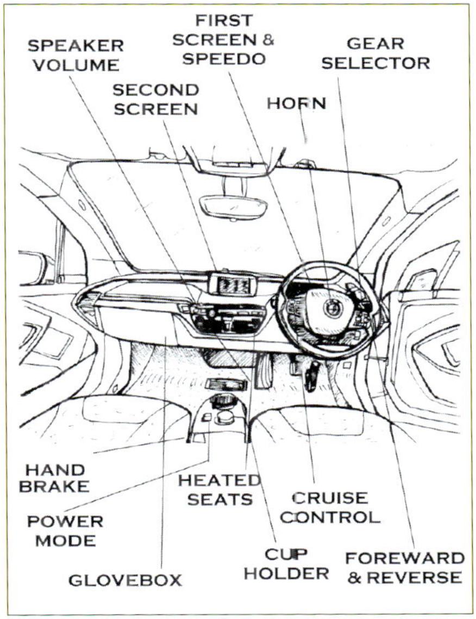

The dashboard of the i3.

Much use was made of aluminium with plastic body panels to keep the weight of this four-seater down. The battery was a sodium-nickel chloride type, unlike the lithium-ion type used three decades later, but range was still a pretty decent 150 miles or so. The model was rear-wheel drive, keeping traditional BMW values alive, with a motor sited at the back. German

The author's i3 range extender in 2017, at a famous 1960s James Bond location in Switzerland.

The author's car photographed on the hottest day ever in France in 2018, with Mont-Saint-Michel in the background. It was around 43°C!

magazine *Auto Zeitung* voted the BMW E1 the winner in the category 'Environment and Technology'. Sadly, a prototype E1 caught fire when charging overnight, which also destroyed much of a building, somewhat tarnishing its reputation.

The i3 and the i8 made their early debut at the 2009 Frankfurt Motor Show in prototype form, with production promised within two years. Interestingly, the i8 displayed was fitted with a three-cylinder diesel engine, which of course never made it into production, although the idea of regenerative braking made its way into both models in production. Both i3 and i8 concepts were remarkably similar to later production examples, although the i3 MCV (Mega City Vehicle) on display was more of a coupé. Further incarnations of the i3 concept were displayed at the Los Angeles Auto Show in 2012, including a five-door hatchback that was adopted, and that rather space age-looking three-door coupé. The new hatch seen the year before at the Frankfurt show had a very low swage line for the extended side windows, allowing greater visibility of the very space-age interior on show, plus a rather stunning yet funky space-age interior which would have been impractical to manufacture. A new UK dealer at Park Lane, London, also had this model on display during the London Olympics.

The i3

From the outset, the i3 was announced as a full plug-in 60Ah electric vehicle, with a 170hp electric motor driving the rear wheels from (initially) an 18kWh battery good for 60-90 miles through low-rolling-resistance, skinny Bridgestone tyres that needed a higher inflation pressure than conventional cars. The i3 production vehicle was launched on 29 July 2013 at New York, London and Beijing after late summer production

An unusually coloured i3 seen traversing the Monte Carlo streets in 2024.

White i3s normally attract the Star Wars movie nickname of 'Storm Trooper'. This is in Monte Carlo again, where it is ideal transport.

and a press launch in Amsterdam. It cost over £30,000 in the UK, but prices were brought down greatly via government incentives to the public to persuade greener travel. Indeed, the i3 won both the World Green Car of the Year and the World Car Design of the Year in 2014, and other awards were won in Australia, the US and South Africa.

An interesting feature of the i3 was the subject of sustainability; most of the interior is made from recycled material such as hemp on the door cards and dashboard top which is mixed with plastic that aids strength at a cost of 10 per cent to the weight. It has to be seen to be believed,

The i3 and rapid charging in France. Its maximum seems slow now at 50kW.

Police forces in Europe have found faithful city service with the i3, including Vatican City.

The last few i3s off the production line. The one in front is the 250,000th built.

but looks good. Even the wooden features on the more lavishly trimmed versions are from certified cultivation in Europe. Another nod in the direction of sports, the first production car was handed over to German marathon runner Jan Fitschen, as it had been used for publicity as a marathon lead vehicle, and the factory only just kept up with demand by manufacturing 70 vehicles a day, soon increasing to 120 at the Leipzig production facility that used i3 700 batteries and wind power to largely electrify the factory.

From the outset, an optional 'range extender' hybrid version had a handy two-gallon fuel tank up front and 647cc Kymco-built twin-cylinder motorcycle engine – as fitted to the BMW C650 GT Maxi Scooter – mounted under the rear boot floor that essentially was an onboard generator for the battery, even when the vehicle was being driven. This model was identified by two fuel flaps, the electric at rear and petrol up front, and overall weighed in at an extra 120kg, cutting down on available payloads somewhat. The range extender engine could be electrically switched on when the HV battery dipped below 75 per cent on European versions and came on automatically at 7 per cent on certain US versions (and European cars) when it reached that low level of charge. This was handy for those early adopters that bought these cars as the charging infrastructure was somewhat limited at the time, although most of the charge points in their infancy were at least free of charge to use.

While the range extender has often been referred to as unreliable and noisy, the author has covered 72,000 miles from new in his 2017 and only detects a slight hum from the rear end with its occasional use, windows closed, and for reliability, it has proved faultless and still produces the same battery range of when it was brand new. Three basic trim types were offered in Europe: Loft, Lodge and Suite. There was also an optional sunroof, in reality, rarely seen. All models came with a central screen information centre, while the more plush models received a wider screen, complementing the standard binnacle in front of the driver, plus a better sound system, privacy glass and leather upholstery. The car was strictly a four-seater with split folding rear seating and a fantastic turning circle on its skinny tyres.

By the time of the 2017 mode , the i3 battery was upgraded to 33kW (BMW confusingly called this their 94Ah model) which gave around 100-140 miles of useful range, although it was outside temperature and speed-dependent. In the US, where legislation dictated that some of the fuel tank had to be blocked off, the effective range was increased by allowing a full tank of fuel – around 10 litres or so. There were no noticeable improvements to the outside or alternative badging either, making it pretty hard to identify a later, longer-range model. Improvements would have to wait for the 2019 model. At around this time the optional rapid charge facility had been standardised, identified by a bigger twin-charging CCS socket behind the rear flap. The CCS was a bold move, as other manufacturers such as Nissan and Renault were adopting different styles of charge ports, but history has proved the CCS is the preferred standard these days.

Within a year, the i3's battery was upgraded to 42kW with the 120Ah model in 2018, and the range extender version was deleted in most markets except for the US. The bumpers were updated to give the car a more aggressive look.

By the end of 2019 – the i3's most successful sales year with around 39,500 sold – an 'S' version was made available with lowered suspension, extra chrome trim on the rear-glass tailgate below the lights and a more sporty appearance and wider track. Much of the rest of the chrome was blacked out, and its modifications weighed in at an extra 20kg.

There were a few 33kW S models manufactured with the range extender. Limited editions included the Unique Forever model in 2022, and the individually painted (tuxedo blue with white accent) by craftsmen Mr Porter model in 2016, which came with a unique travel kit including an i-leather holdall, a Leica camera, Cutler and Cross sunglasses, Lock and Co bowler hat and a specially printed Phaidon city guidebook. The car cost £43,500! Normal production continued to mid-2024, when the model was deleted with ten special final units produced in frozen grey or frozen red II paint. The lucky owners had pre-ordered and saw their cars being built, each equipped with Harmon Kardon hi-fi, professional navigation, park assistance control, and leather instrument panel. Interiors were all in Vernasca dark truffle upholstery.

Comparative values have held up well compared with its earlier rivals, the Nissan Leaf and Renault Zoe, and the motoring press believe that this car will become a future classic. In the US/UK the i3 was available in the following trim types:

Mega World (cloth seats and 19in wheels) – Atelier in UK

Giga World (leather seat inserts and uprated 19in wheels) – Lodge in the UK

Tera World (full leather and upgraded 428 alloy wheels) – Suite in the UK

Note: wheel types were not locked into trim options in the UK.

i3 BODY TYPES: Five-door hatchback, four-seat only. **Manufactured at:** Leipzig (Germany). **Number produced:** 250,000. **Production span:** 2013-2024.
PERFORMANCE: Top speed: 94mph/150km/h; **0-60mph/100km/h:** 7 seconds; **average economy:** 3-5 miles/kWh.
PRICE AT LAUNCH: £30,680.
MEASUREMENTS: Length: 13ft 0in (3.99m); **height:** 4ft 4½in (1.59m); **width:** 6ft 8in (2.03m); **wheelbase:** 7ft 1 n (2.57m); **kerb weight:** 2650lb (1195kg); **wheels:** 19in alloy; **turning circle:** 28ft 4in (10.3m); **fuel capacity:** 2 gallons/9 litres (on Rex version only); **boot capacity:** 260/1100 litres (seats up/down).
TECHNICAL: Engine types (on Range Extender version): 647cc two-cylinder petrol, electric motor; **suspension:** MacPherson strut coil front, five-link coil springs rear; **brakes:** disc front and rear.
TRIM: Cloth or leather.
KEY OPTIONAL EXTRAS: Sunroof, privacy glass, reversing camera, 20in wheels, wider infotainment screen, range extender, leather seats, driving assistant plus.

i3 advertising slogans

As promised. The all-electric BMW i3.
The new BMW i3. Born to go further.
BMW i. Born electric. (Showroom banner with i8)
The BMW i3 and i3s. Born electric.
Tomorrow. Today.
Drive the future now.
Hello future.
Lead the charge. Some fear change, others drive it.
Driven by innovation. And electricity.
Drive to feel the energy.
... and helps to give back to the environment.

The i8

The revolutionary BMW i8 sports car was launched in the summer of 2014, several months after initially being shown as a Richard Kim-designed concept car at the previous Frankfurt Motor Show. This model, alongside the i3, stunned the crowds with its butterfly doors (not quite the gullwing types seen on the 1970s Bricklin and the Delorean back in 1981). It was only ever marketed as a plug-in hybrid, and it was fitted with a 1499cc centrally mounted three-cylinder turbo petrol engine, and a much smaller 7.1kWh lithium-ion battery powering a front-mounted electric motor through the front wheels for zero-emissions use in cities where required and to aid in economy. This size battery would give approximately 20 to 25 miles of silent range.

The unique flip-up doors of the i8.

With its all-wheel drive, performance through the six-speed transmission was startling, with road testers achieving a limited 155mph with 0-60mph figures of 4.4 seconds, well approaching Tesla and supercar

The i8 saloon and roadster at an RAF Bentwaters EV day in Suffolk, 2018.

Protonic blue was a popular i3 and i8 colour choice.

The i8 roadster test model the author drove at RAF Bentwaters at a 'very high speed' on the long and wide private runway.

territory. In May 2018, a cabriolet/roadster model was produced, its design having been seen initially at the 2012 Beijing Motor Show as the roadster concept, and this, and the hardtop version which continued, had a 11.6kWh battery with a revised electric range of between 30 to 35 miles.

An interesting feature of the i8 was the option of turning on internal combustion engine noises when on the move. Having enthusiastically track tested such a brand-new example on the large and wide Bentwaters airfield in Suffolk in 2018, the author found this feature a little quirky to get used to. The hardest thing was getting in and out of the low cabin, but having transgressed straight from my already quick i3, I certainly had a refreshed smile on my face!

Marketing was surprisingly strong for such a limited-build car, and several model manufacturers made die cast and plastic models of the i8, and even toddler sit-in cars became available in 6-volt! An interesting footnote is that a large billboard poster was displayed in towns and cities soon after launch, no doubt appealing to all 1980s kids, now grown up with their own money to spend. The i8 was compared to a gullwing Delorean, displayed on the left with the caption "2015. Roads, where we're going we don't need roads." On the right, facing the Delorean sat an i8 with the headline "2014. How cute. BMW i. Born electric" – certain references to the *Back to the Future* sci-fi movie trilogy.

In all, 20,465 i8 units were sold to markets in Australia, India, Mexico, Indonesia, the US, Europe and Thailand up to its demise in June 2020, which is a lot less than the sister BMW i3 car described above that sold around a quarter of a million units, but it did make the model the world's top-selling electric sports car, beating the much earlier and almost forgotten Tesla Roadster by some margin. The special edition of the range was the Protonic Red model, unveiled at the Geneva International Motor Show in 2016. The car had W-spoke 470 light-alloy wheels in orbit grey metallic, with the interior trim gaining

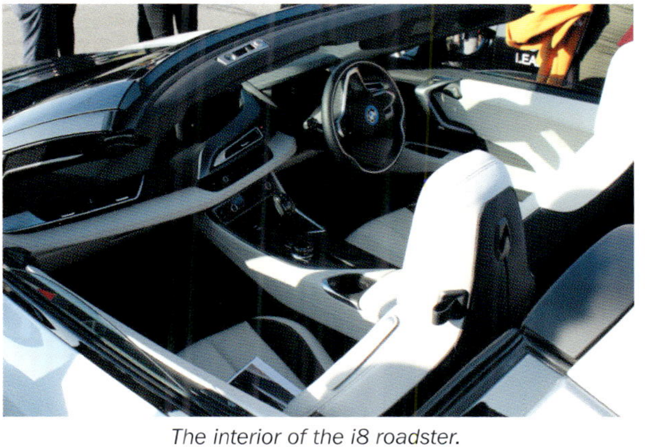

The interior of the i8 roadster.

The rear aspect of the i8 coupé.

red double stitching and other trim in carbon fibre and ceramics. The bodywork was finished in Protonic Red with accents in Frozen Grey. Another notable extra was the exclusive Louis Vuitton Carbon Black luggage sold throughout their key stores throughout the globe from 2014 on.

i8 advertising slogans
BMW i. Born electric
Icon of a new era
Electrify your future
Science not fiction
Surreal impressionist
The sustainable supercar
The world's power supply
Ultimate driving machine
24 hours to the future
Flowing brilliance
Once a notion. Now a reality
Straight from the twilight zone
Sustain the environment. Expand the enjoyment
The legacy drives on
The performance to go fast. The technology to go far

i8 BODY TYPES: Two-door coupé (four-seat), two-door convertible (two-seat). **Manufactured at:** Leipzig Germany. **Number produced:** 20,465 (16,581 coupés and 3884 roadsters). **Production span:** 2014-2020.
PERFORMANCE: Top speed: 155mph/250km/h; **0-60mph/100km/h:** 4.2 seconds; **average economy:** 40-45mpg.
PRICE AT LAUNCH: £99,845.
MEASUREMENTS: Length: 12ft 11in (4.69m); **height:** 4ft 3in (1.29m); **width:** 6ft 4½in (1.94m); **wheelbase:** 9ft 2in (2.8m); **kerb weight:** 3394lb (1539kg); **wheels:** 20in alloy; **turning circle:** 33ft 10in (12.3m); **fuel capacity:** 9.2 gallons/42 litres; **boot capacity:** 154 litres.
TECHNICAL: Engine types: 1499cc three-cylinder petrol plus electric motor; **gearbox:** six-speed automatic (petrol) two-speed (electric motor); **suspension:** coil front and rear; **brakes:** disc front and rear.
TRIM: Leather.

The future's electric …

This book covers up to the beginning of the i3 and i8 era only, but many more electric cars have been produced since, including a wide variety of hybrids. Some models are quite a bit larger as battery technology has developed, with greater power storage available at the same size, while being cheaper to produce. Later saloon cars were also available as hybrids for those customers not willing to change completely to electric power, with the existing internal combustion motor still turning the wheels, unlike the i3's range extender 'onboard generator', an idea soon successfully adopted by some London taxis.

The i8 can be driven as pure electric, pure petrol, or both for rapid acceleration!

APPENDIX 1

E-series model designations explained

Most of the BMW range has largely, for the past few decades at least, used similar boot badge designations, albeit 3, 5, 6 or 7 Series. For some dedicated enthusiasts the E-series names seem to flow off the tongue with ease, and with others, a problem often exists to identify which specific model is which. This list presents the E-series designations in number order to form this quick reference guide. Those listed are the ones that made it to production; missing numbers may well be down to aborted projects and shelved ideas. The production years of the relevant models are also included for clarity, and these E numbers appear at the start of each section of this book. Incidentally, E stands for 'entwicklung' (German for 'development').

Series	Models	Production span
E3	2500, 2800, 3.0 & 3.3Li	1968-1977
E6/12	02 Series	1967-1977
E9	Coupés, 2000, 2800, 3.0	1965-1975
E10	Touring version of 02	1967-1977
E12	(1st) 5 Series	1972-1981
E20	2002 Tii & Turbo	1967-1977
E21	(1st) 3 Series	1975-1983
E23	(1st) 7 Series	1977-1987
E24	(1st) 6 Series	1977-1989
E25	Turbo concept car	1972
E26	M1	1978-1981
E28	(2nd) 5 Series	1982-1988
E30	(2nd) 3 Series & Z1	1982-1991
E31	8 Series	1989-1999
E32	(2nd) 7 Series	1986-1994
E34	(3rd) 5 Series	1988-1996
E36	(3rd) 3 Series	1990-1998
E36/7	Z3	1996-2002
E38	(3rd) 7 Series	1993-2001
E39	(4th) 5 Series	1995-2004
E46	(4th) 3 Series	1998-2005
E52	Z8 Roadster	1999-2003
E53	(1st) X5	1999-2006
E60	(5th) 5 Series	2003-2010
E61	(5th) 5 Series Touring	2003-2010
E63	(2nd) 6 Series coupé	2003-2010
E64	(2nd) 6 Series convertible	2004-2010
E65	(4th) 7 Series	2001-2008
E66	(4th) 7 Series LWB	2002-2008
E70	(2nd) X5	2006-2013
E71	X6	2008-2014
E81	1 Series (3-door)	2007-2012
E82	1 Series (coupé)	2007-2014
E83	X3	2003-2010
E84	X1	2009-2015
E85	Z4	2002-2008
E86	Z4 coupé	2006-2008
E87	1 Series (5-door)	2004-2011
E88	1 Series convertible	2007-2013
E89	Z4	2009-2016
E90	(5th) 3 Series saloon	2005-2011
E91	(5th) 3 Series estate	2005-2011
E92	(5th) 3 Series coupé	2006-2013
E93	(5th) 3 Series convertible	2006-2013

APPENDIX 2

Key achievements in motorsport

There have been a high number of race wins and entries across the globe with BMW products, from club racing through to the Le Mans 24 Hours and the ETCC. Enjoy this photographic array of historic BMW cars used in motorsport.

The Schnitzer/ Motul 2800 CS.

A works 700 competing on the Monte Carlo Rally of 1961, seen here at Monaco.

Below: M1 cars competing at Monaco in 1979 in the Procar event.

The works X3 won the Alcan Winter Rally in 2004, seen here battling the heavy snow.

The M30 E30 raced with the BMW M Team.

The 2002 taking part in the Touring Car Championship in 1969.

A furiously driven 600 takes part in the Tauernringfahrt in 1959.

The 3 Series quickly became known as the world's most successful Touring Car on the race scene. A Warsteiner sponsored M3 shown here on the track.

The racing E9 CSL on display in a German museum.

A mid 1970s German advertisement depicting the CSL.

Mobil oils were quick to advertise their products in the early 1990s, this advert shows the M3.

Mountain champion Hans Stuck in his 700 RS in 1961 (Austrian Hill Climbing Championship).

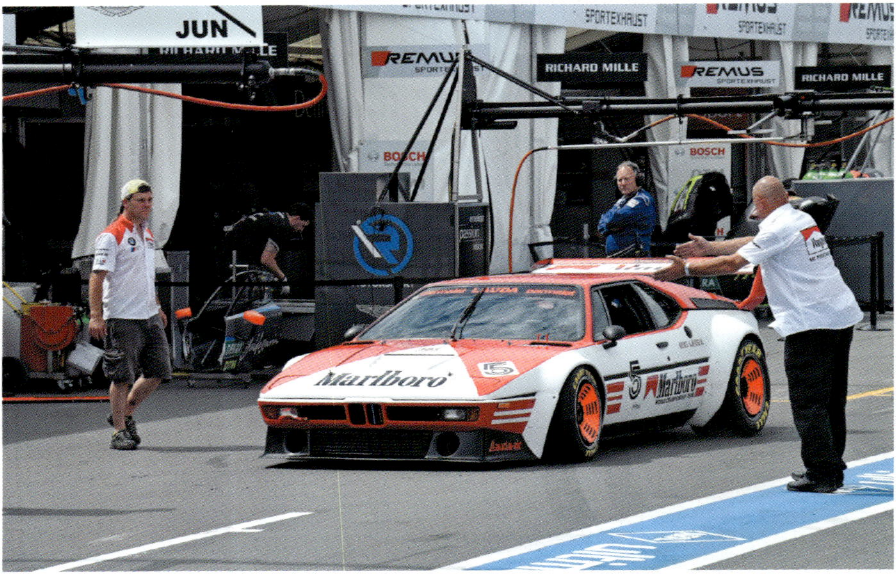

The Procar revival, and the M1 in 1979 enters the pits.

The Hervé Poulain/Manfred Winkelhock M1 race car in action; it finished sixth at Le Mans in 1979. The car still survives in its distinctive Andy Warhol colours and was subject to a flour-throwing attack by activists at the Fabbrica del Vapore exhibition in Milan in November 2022. The car was then stated to be worth £50,000,000!

APPENDIX 3

BMW TV and movie appearances

If you want to see BMWs driving in TV shows or in the movies, this section is for you. Cars are often an integral part of a TV or film production, and often become stars in their own right, with surviving vehicles often cherished by their modern-day owners. Look around any major classic car show and you will see at least one car made famous by studio work, often with life-size cardboard cutouts alongside of the relevant actors.

If a BMW has made a key appearance, or perhaps been in a police car chase on TV or the silver screen, it should be listed here. Most of the appearances listed are in English-speaking productions, although when a key model has not been found within this scope, some overseas films and TV appearances are also included. Often the specific model designation is unknown, indicated by just the relevant model series making the entry more generic. Of course this list is not exhaustive; there are simply thousands of BMWs on the screen, many just making a brief appearance, and space limitations here make it impossible to list them all.

Of course it is great to see BMWs in blockbuster, and now truly classic, films. For example, the heavily customised matt black and orange hovercraft convertible of character Biff (or futuristic Griff in this instance) in *Back to the Future II* was actually a radically altered and roof-chopped European specification E24 1976 633 CSI complete with E21 tail lamps. This was painstakingly restored to its film appearance quite a few years later by an American enthusiast who drove miles to acquire it in 2004.

The Hire is a group of eight movies each of 10 minutes all staring Clive Owen and a selection of contemporary BMW cars, and was available to download and watch on the official BMW website in 2001/2002. The DVD set (produced on three separate occasions by BMW to meet the heavy demand) can command a premium price on the second-hand market now and is well worth a look. Clive Owen is our driver sampling a broad spectrum of new BMWs in a very secret-agent, action-man way. The concept of the content of these short films had come from the 1998 movie *Ronin* (already well respected for its car chases) and afterwards the series inspired *The Transporter* movies with Jason Statham. There, Statham is seen in a heavily reworked black E38 735i, fitted with the V12 engine of the 750 but unusually with manual transmission. There are impressive stunts and spectacular action, all worth watching.

Product placement by BMW led to the new Z3 appearing in a 007 James Bond movie instead of the regular Aston Martin or Lotus that the character Q had previously prepared for our hero, now played by a new actor: Pierce Brosnan. In *GoldenEye,* the Z3 was only used in a couple of scenes despite all the media hype shown ahead of the film, but it certainly helped sales of the new model, and actor Desmond Llewellyn, who played Q, was at the vehicle's launch in 1995. The two following James Bond movies also included BMWs as key cars for Brosnan, with *Tomorrow Never Dies* in 1997 having a remote-controlled E38 750iL driven at speed against a Senator in an underground car park. A UK-registered and titanium-armoured Z8 (V354FMP) was in *The World is not Enough* in 1999. The latter film saw the Z8 spectacularly cut in half by a large industrial saw mounted on a helicopter, and sliced lengthways! Only 16 pre-production prototypes had been built at the time of filming, and the film's producers wanted 12 of them – and most had no engines, but all went well, and the launch of the Z8 coincided with the release of the film in November 1999.

The Bond equipment fitted to the Z8 included:

- Rocket motor
- Machine guns
- Smoke screen facility
- Surface-to-air missiles
- EMP generator to disable nearby electrical devices.

The sliced shell now forms part of a James Bond feature in a museum, and model kit manufacturer Revell produced an attractive 1:24 scale model of the car made of 69 parts. Another silver Z8 – a 5-litre version registered in September 2000 – survives to this day with this number plate having covered less than miles from new ...

An interesting anecdote by Rowan Atkinson's character in the 2018 movie *Johnny English Strikes Again* was the comment on an enemy driving a white i3 in the Alps just before taking chase. "Look sir, it's one of those new electric cars!" commented his side-kick Boff. "It sounds like a nose hair trimmer ... A bunch of triple A batteries is no match for good old-fashioned British horsepower!" Shortly after, ironically, our hero ran out of petrol in his Aston Martin! In real life, Rowan Atkinson actually drove around London in his own BMW i3. Incidentally, an American TV and cinema advert ran soon after the launch of the i3 depicting one driving silently around a public library, the point being it was so quiet it would not disturb the readers.

This TV and film list below largely covers vehicles within the date scope of this book. They are worth looking out for on YouTube, streaming online or in old DVD stores and on eBay! For further research, look at imcdb.org online for a fascinating glimpse of all manufacturers, including motorcycle and commercials.

Earliest models

327 – *Lola* (1981)
328 – *Easy Virtue* (1936)
501 – *Look at Life: Eyes of the Law* (1962)
502 – *Harlis* (1972)
502 – *The American Success Company* (1980)
503 – *The Last Run* (1971)
503 – *Die Rosel Vom Schwarzwald* (1956)
507 – *Fantomas* (1964)

Microcars

Isetta – *Never Let Me Down Again*, Depeche Mode music (1987)
Isetta – *The Naked Truth* (1957)
Isetta – *The Small Escape* (2019)
Isetta – *Family Matters* (TV)
Isetta 250 – *Export Klein Aber Main* (1980)
Isetta 300 – *Family Matters* (TV)
Isetta 300 – *How to Make a Doll* (1968)
Isetta Export – *Stahlnetz – Saison* (1961)
600 micro – *Klein aber Mein* (1980)
700 cabrio – *Cabin Fever* (1969)

1960s/early 1970s cars

1500 – *Inklusive Totenscheim* (1977)
1600 Cabrio – *La Nuit Americaine* (1973)
1600 GT – *Betão Ronca Ferro* (1970)
1600 Ti – *Auf Achse* (TV)
1600-2 – *The Swiss Conspiracy* (1976)
1602 – *The Salzburg Connection* (1972)
1800 – *Der Kommissar* (TV)
1802 – *Requiem* (2006)
2000 CS – *Man in a Suitcase*
2000 CS – *Le Cerveau* (1969)
2000 tilux – *Vampyres* (1974)
2000 tilux – *Mission Impossible* (TV)
2002 – *Neutral* (2017)
2002 – *The Squeeze* (1977)
2002 – *Try Seventeen* (2002)
2002 – *The China Syndrome* (1979)
2002 tii – *Autobahnraser* (2004)
2002 Touring – *L'emmerdeur*
2002 Turbo – *Car S.O.S.* (TV)
2500 (E3) – *Der Kommissar*
2500 (E3) – *The Fall Guy*
2500 (E3) – *The Persuaders*
2800 (E3) – *Der Vorgang* (1973)
2800 CS (E9) – *Derrick* (TV)
3.0 L (E3) – *L'homme Presse* (1977)
3.0 S (E3) – *The New Avengers* (TV)
3.0 Si (E3) – *Man at the Top*
3.0 CS (E9) – *Fracture* (2007)
3.0 CSL (E9) – *Circuit no Okami* (1977)
3.0 CSi (E9) – *The Art of Racing in the Rain* (2019)
3200 CS (532) – *Das ist Stern Schnuppe* (1965)
3.3 Li (E3) – *Comme un Boomerang* (1976)

1 Series

1M (E82) – *The Gambler*
1 Series (E87) – *The Day of the Jackal* (2024)
118i (E87) – *Criminal Record* (TV)
135i Cabriolet (E88) – *The Lying Game*

3 Series

316i (E30) – *The Breaker Upperers* (2018)
316 ti Compact (E46/5) – *Life in the Balance* (2003)
318i Cabrio (E36) – *T2 Trainspotting* (2017)
320 (E21) – *Defence of the Realm* (1979)
320d (E90) – *Northern Lights* (2006)
320i (E21) – *Halloween* (1978)

320i (E21) – *Night School* (1981)
320i (E21) – *Penny Dreadful* (2001)
320i (E30) – *Bob & Rose*
320i (E30) – *A Very Peculiar Practice*
320i (E30) – *Collision*
320i Cabrio (E30) – *The Space Between*
320d (E46) – *Five by Five* (TV)
323i Baur Cabrio (E30) – *Comfort and Joy* (1984)
323i (E36) – *A Boyfriend for Christmas* (2004)
323i (E90) – *Secret Liaison* (2013)
325i Cabrio (E30) – *Buffy the Vampire Slayer*
325i Cabrio (E30) – *Beverly Hills, 90210*
325i Baur cabrio (E30) – *Sweet Murder* (1990)
325 iS Coupé (E36) – *The Chase* (1994)
325 xi (E46) – *Chastnik* (2008)
325 xi (E46) – *Lipstick Jungle* (TV)
328i (E36) – *I know What You Did Last Summer* (1997)
328i Coupé – *The Hire: The Follow*
328i (E93) – *Crimes of the Mind* (2014)
328i (E92) – *The Samaritan*
328i (E92) – *Jersey Shore* (TV)
328i Cabrio (E36) – *Frank vs God* (2014)
330 Ci (E46) – *The Follow* (2001)
330 Ci (E46) – *Doctors*
330 Ci (E46) – *The Bling Ring* (2011)
330i ZHP (E46) – *Wheelman* (2017)
M3 Cabriolet (E36) – *Daylight Robbery*
M3 Cabriolet (E46) – *A Trace of Danger* (2010)
M3 (E36) – *Mischief Invasion* (2004)
M3 (F30) – *Mission Impossible (Ghost protocol)*
M Roadster (E36/7) – *Tiff Needell: Burning Rubber* (TV, 2001)
3 Series (E21) – *The Stranger* (1987)
3 Series (E34) – *Drifter* (2014)
3 Series (E36) – *The Chase*
3 Series (E46) – *Need for Speed: Most Wanted*
3 Series (E46) – *Undercover Grandpa* (2017)
3 Series (E46) – *Most!* (TV)
3 Series Touring (E46) – *Wreck* (2020)

5 Series

518 (E28) – *Octopussy*, James Bond (1983)
520 (E12) – *Auf Wiedersehen, Pet*
520 (E12) – *The Turnaround* (1995)
520i (E28) – *The Crying Game* (1992)
520i (E39) – *Cold Feet*
523i (E39) – *The Bill* (TV)
523i (E39) – *Honest* (TV)
525e (E28) – *The Fly* (2015)
525d Touring (E61) – *Espion(s)* (2009)
528i (E12) – *Les Comperes* (1983)
528i (E12) – *Double Threat* (1993)
528i (E28) – *Mission Impossible – Fallout* (2018)
528i (E39) – *Vacancy* (2007)
528i Touring (E39) – *The Bill* (TV)
540i (E39) – *The Possession* (2012)
540i (E39) – *The Hire: Chosen* (2001)
M5 (E39) – *The Hire: Star* (2001)
M5 (E60) – *Fast & Furious 6*
M5 Touring (E61) – *Nobel* (TV)
5 Series – *The Hire* (*The Escape*)
5 Series – *The Bourne Supremacy*
5 Series (E28) – *A Cool, Dry Place* (1998)
5 Series (E34) – *Ronin* (1998)
5 Series (E34) – *Frasier* (TV)
5 Series (E39) – *Murder in Mind* (TV)
5 Series (E39) – *The Last Trimester* (2007)
5 Series (E60) – *The Driver* (2014, TV)
5 Series (E60) – *The Bill* (TV)
5 Series (E60) – *Identity* (2010)

6 Series

630i (E64) – *Race* (2008)
633 CSi (E24) – *Back to the Future II*
633 CSi (E24) – *Dallas* (TV)
635 CSi (E24) – *The Eliminators* (2016)
635 CSi (E24) – *The Black Tower* (1985)
635 CSi (E24) – *A Man Called Hawk* (1989)
M635 CSi (E24) – *Looking After Jo Jo* (TV)
M635 CSi (E24) – *Howards' Way* (TV)
645 Ci (E63) – *Acts of Vengeance* (2017)

7 Series

732i (E23) – *Travelling Man* (1984)
733i (E23) – *Tales of the Unexpected* (1980)
733i (E32) – *Nothing But Trouble* (1991)
735i (E23) – *Lock, Stock* (1983)
735i (E32) – *Speed Zone* (1989)
735i (E38) – *The Transporter* (2002)
740i (E38) – *The Hire: Ambush* (2001)
740iL (E38) – *Fun With Dick & Jane* (2005)
740iL (E38) – *Tomorrow Never Dies*, James Bond (badged as 750) (1997)
745i (E23) – *Texasville* (1990)
745i (E65) – *The Haunted Mansion* (2003)
740iL (E38) – *Tomorrow Never Dies*, James Bond (1997)
750iL (E38) – *The Double* (2011
760 Li (E66) – *Taxi* (2004)
7 Series (E23) – *Loophole* (1981)
7 Series (E23) – *Floodtide* (1980)
7 Series (E32) – *Gladbeck* (2018)
7 Series (E32) – *Zero 2* (2010)

7 Series (E32) – *The One Game* (1988)
7 Series (E32) – *Ripple* (2008)
7 Series – *The Hire* (Ambush)
7 Series – *The Game* (1997)
7 Series (E38) – *Bimmer*
7 Series (E65) – *The Prince & Me II: The Royal Wedding*
7 Series (E70) – *Locke* (2013)
7 Series (E70) – *Babylon* (2014)
7 Series (E70) – *The Ghost Writer* (2010)

8 Series

840 Ci (E31) – *Chauffeur de Maitre* (1996)
850i – *The Score*
850i (E31) – *Eyes of the Beholder* (1992)
850 CSi (E31) – *Psycho Diver: Masei Rakuryu* (1997)

4x4

X1 (E84) – *Broken Trust* (2012)
X1 (E84) – *Stolen From the Suburbs* (2015)
X3 (E83) – *No Brother of Mine* (2007)
X5 – *The Hire: Powder Keg*
X5 (E53) – *Momentum* (2015)
X5 (E53) – *Dark Harvest* (2016)
X5 (E53) – *Everwood* (TV)
X5 (E53) – *Horseplay* (2003)
X5 M50d – *Locke* (2013)

Electric

i3 (I01) – *M3GAN* (2022)
i3 (I01) – *Extant* (TV, 2014/5)
i3 (I01) – *Johnny English Strikes Again* (2018)
i3 (I01) – *Lethal Weapon*
i3 (I01) – *Curb Your Enthusiasm* (TV)
i8 (I12) – *Mission Impossible (Ghost protocol)*
i8 (I12) – *Late Shift* (2016)
i8 (I12) – *Little* (2019)
i8 Roadster (I15) – *Riviera*
i8 Roadster (I15) – *Shameless* (US TV series)

M1

M1 (E26) – *Speed Driver* (1980)

Z-series

Z1 (E30Z) – *Der Checker* (TV)
Z1 (E30Z) – *Clarkson's Top 100 Cars* (TV, 2001)
Z3 – *GoldenEye*, James Bond (1995)
Z3 (E36/7) – *The Hire: The Follow* (2001)
Z3 – *72 Heures* (2005)
Z4 (E85) – *The Hire: (Hostage, Ticker & Beat the Devil)*
Z4 (E85) – *It Takes a Man and a Woman* (2013)
Z4 (E85) – *Flirting with Danger* (2006)
Z4 (E86) – *Fast Track: No Limits* (2008)
Z8 – *The World Is Not Enough,* James Bond (1999)

A Pictorial History

more in the series

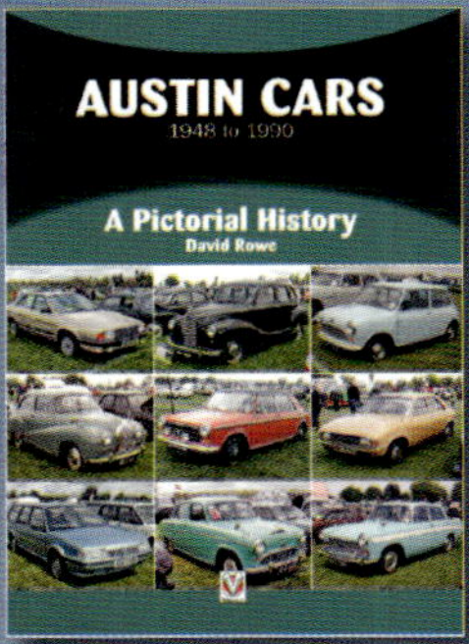

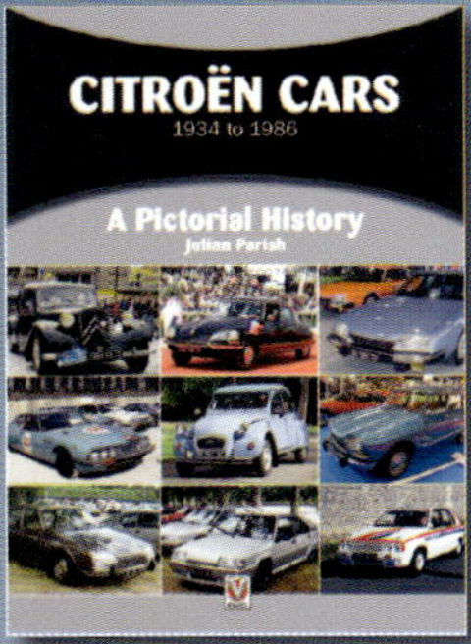

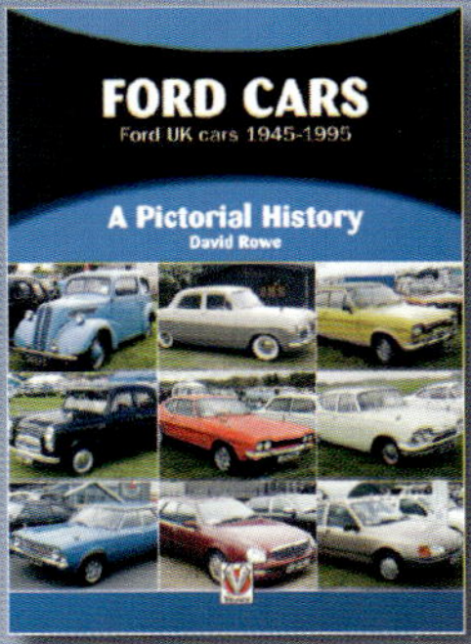

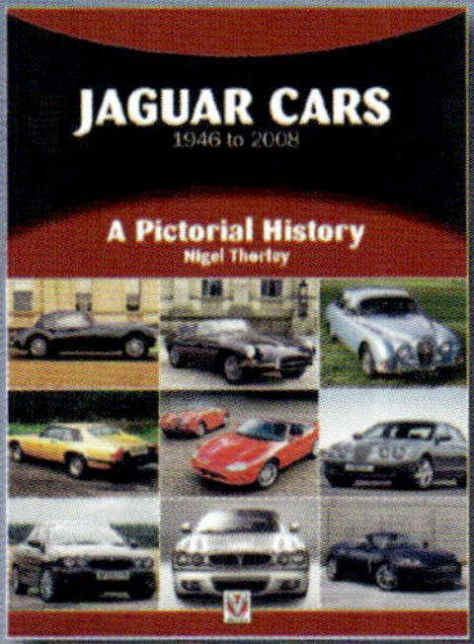

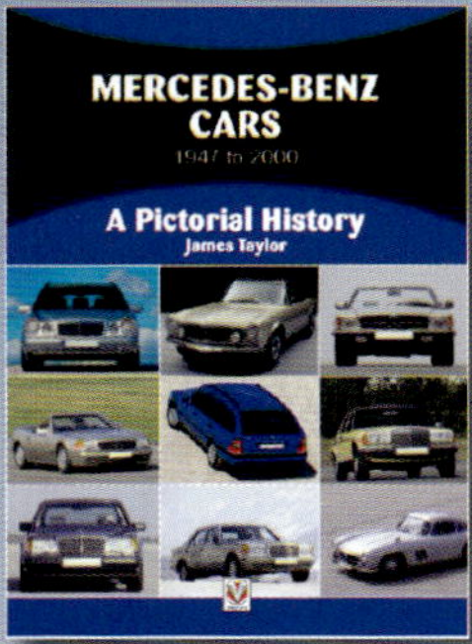

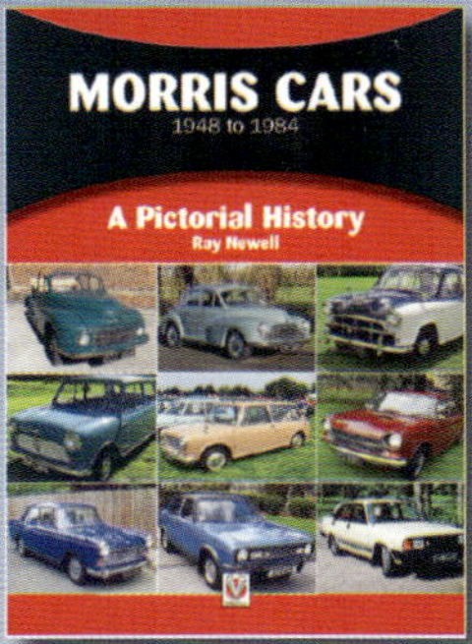

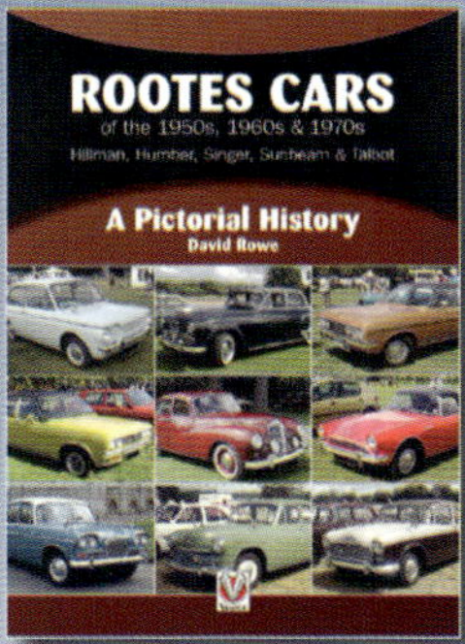

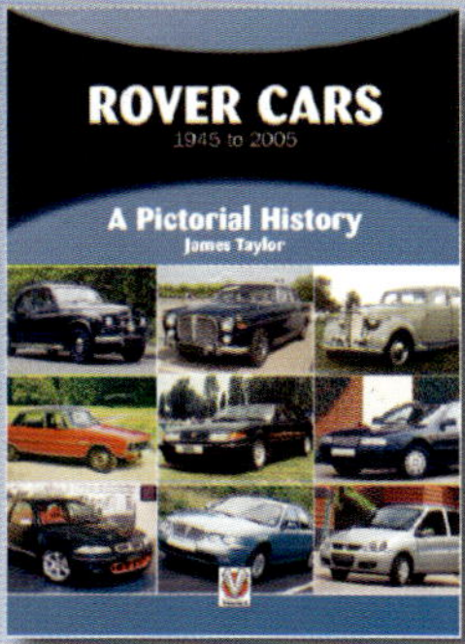

These handy reference books cover all the key models, providing an overview of history and car design, detailed technical specifications and production data, all illustrated with hundreds of colour photographs and informative diagrams.

To see the full range of Pictorial Histories see www.veloce.co.uk

INDEX

I am indebted to my friend Nasir Salek for his help and guidance with this book, particularly concerning the more modern cars that I discovered had challenging model line ups. Nasir has owned and driven many BMWs over the years. I am seen here on the left, alongside my i3 REx, a car purchased from new with a view to keeping it forever, now at 8 years old and with a trouble free 72,000 miles. On the right is Nasir with his sixth generation 3 Series, a stunning 2015 BMW F30 330d Xdrive Msport. The cars are wildly different to each other, but both cared for and driven by keen enthusiasts.